What people are saying about …

FAITH PATH
WORKBOOK AND DVD

"Mark has emerged as a well-reasoned voice in the conversation about faith."

Max Lucado, best-selling author of *3:16: The Numbers of Hope*

"Embark on a journey of spiritual discovery, and let Mark's remarkable insights revolutionize your life."

Lee Strobel, best-selling author of *The Case for the Real Jesus*

"I have a dream!—every church in America going through this incredibly insightful and stimulating course by Mark Mittelberg on the real meaning of faith. This could sow the seeds of revival for generations—that's how good and important this training is."

Dr. Craig J. Hazen, founder and director of the graduate program in Christian apologetics at Biola University, and author of the novel *Five Sacred Crossings*

"As believers, we know it is essential to share our faith with those we care about and love. But because we lack confidence, we often shy away from communicating the gospel. Mark's *Faith Path* curriculum will help you understand the six paths your friends are currently on and give you the confidence to share your faith with them—with amazing results. I highly recommend *Faith Path* as an outreach training tool for believers and churches!"

Scott Evans, president and CEO of Outreach

"Mark Mittelberg is one of the world's leading lights when it comes to equipping Christians for authentic, loving, and intelligent evangelistic efforts. Yet when you watch the *Faith Path* DVD, you'll feel like he's a trusted friend sitting right next to you! This resource is great for small groups, seminars, and Sunday school classes—to help you discover the fun and fulfillment of sharing your faith with others."

Michael R. Licona, PhD, apologetics coordinator for the North American Mission Board of the Southern Baptist Convention, and coauthor of *The Case for the Resurrection of Jesus*

"Want to have great conversations about God with your unchurched friends and family? You'll want to understand their faith path! It's all here: Mark's insights on the six common ways people choose what to believe, real-life testimonies from people who were on each of the six paths, and great questions that enable captivating discussions within your small group. The result: You'll be equipped for kingdom-building interactions with almost anyone!"

Mary Schaller, president of Q Place (QPlace.com), and author of *How to Start a Q Place*

"Mark has done it again. He has shaped a resource that will become a standard in training Christians to reach out to others with the grace and truth of Jesus. *Faith Path* will prepare you for a journey of walking with spiritually curious friends right where they are, in the unique ways God has wired them. It is natural and organic, and it works!"

Kevin G. Harney, author of *Organic Outreach for Ordinary People*

FAITH PATH

WORKBOOK

FAITH PATH

HELPING FRIENDS FIND THEIR WAY TO CHRIST

MARK MITTELBERG

David C Cook®
transforming lives together

FAITH PATH
Published by David C. Cook
4050 Lee Vance View
Colorado Springs, CO 80918 U.S.A.

David C. Cook Distribution Canada
55 Woodslee Avenue, Paris, Ontario, Canada N3L 3E5

David C. Cook U.K., Kingsway Communications
Eastbourne, East Sussex BN23 6NT, England

David C. Cook and the graphic circle C logo
are registered trademarks of Cook Communications Ministries.

Unless otherwise indicated, all Scripture quotations are taken from the *Holy Bible, New Living Translation*,
copyright © 1996, 2004. Used by permission of Tyndale House Publishers, Inc., Wheaton, Illinois 60189. All
rights reserved. Scripture quotations marked NIV are taken from the *Holy Bible, New International Version*®. NIV®.
Copyright © 1973, 1978, 1984 International Bible Society. Used by permission of Zondervan. All rights reserved.

References taken from *Choosing Your Faith* published by Tyndale in
2008 © Mark Mittelberg, ISBN 978-1-4143-1579-9.

ISBN 978-1-4347-6513-0

© 2009 Mark Mittelberg

Published in association with the literary agency of Alive Communications, Inc,
7680 Goddard St., Suite 200, Colorado Springs, CO 80920

The Team: Brian Thomasson, Karen Lee-Thorp, Sarah Schultz, Jack Campbell, and Karen Athen
Cover Design: Amy Kiechlin
Cover Photo: iStockphoto

Printed in the United States of America
First Edition 2009

2 3 4 5 6 7 8 9 10

010510

To Stuart C. Hackett, my professor, mentor, and friend—and truly one of the brightest minds on the planet. Thank you for your lifelong commitment to teaching the truth, and to making the One who *is* the Truth known to many.

CONTENTS

INTRODUCTION

Many Christians cringe at the thought of talking with non-Christians about faith. Often it feels like discussing music with someone who's tone deaf or trying to explain the color green to a person born blind. Maybe they're happily practicing the religion they grew up with or they're into some form of spirituality we don't entirely understand. Or perhaps they go so far as to think religion and spirituality are the pastimes of fools. Regardless, we can sometimes feel like fools trying to point them toward Christ and his incredible gift of salvation.

Still, whether they believe it or not, there is nothing more important for their lives and futures than the question of how they'll respond to God and his amazing grace. It really matters. And if we care about our friends, we want nothing more than to help them avoid disastrous mistakes. We want them to know Christ and to experience the forgiveness, leadership, and new life he offers. So what can we do?

One important thing we can do is to try to first understand them. We can listen to them and discover how they think and how they arrived at their current points of view. Then we'll be in a better position to help them rethink their conclusions and to point them toward the truths of the Christian faith.

The fact is, people are not all the same. They consider and weigh spiritual matters in differing ways. In other words, they're on a variety of *faith paths*. One person might say, "I believe what I do because I was raised with that belief." Another relies on mystical feelings and experiences. Another wants logic and evidence; yet another says, "Why do I need your evidence when my heart tells me what to believe?"

This workbook and its accompanying DVD are about helping your friends consider and choose the beliefs they will live by, with the hope of ultimately leading them to faith in Christ. This training series will help you:

- Understand people who approach life differently from you

- Recognize the danger of paths that can lead away from Christ

- Deepen your own faith in Christ and reinforce your reasons for believing

- Gain confidence in talking about Christ with others

You're going to meet six individuals who looked at the world in very different ways before they embraced faith in Christ. They were on the six different faith paths. Very likely you'll recognize people you know in these six ways of thinking. You may even recognize yourself. Through the stories of these individuals, as well as the discussions that follow, you'll learn how to help people like them overcome their barriers to trusting in Christ.

And here's what's ironic: Helping people wisely choose their faith will not only serve *them* throughout their lives and into eternity—but you'll also discover that doing so can become the greatest adventure in your *own* life!

There is simply nothing more exhilarating or rewarding than helping people you love meet the God who loves them.

HOW TO GET THE MOST
OUT OF THIS WORKBOOK

This workbook is designed to be used in a group with the *Faith Path* DVD. If you use it in a small group of up to twelve people, you can discuss the questions together as one group. If you're in a larger class than that, you may find it beneficial to subdivide into discussion circles of four or five people. Then everyone will have plenty of time to share their thoughts.

> *See the Leader's Guide at the end of this workbook for details on how to facilitate this. The Leader's Guide is intended for the small-group leader or class teacher. However, if you're leading a discussion circle of four or five people, you will find the Leader's Guide helpful too.*

Faith Path is linked to the book *Choosing Your Faith* by Mark Mittelberg (Tyndale, 2008). This book is written to encourage you. It's also designed for you to give to your friends who don't yet know Christ. Many of the concepts in *Choosing Your Faith* are echoed in this workbook and on the DVD. But often we can hit only the highlights here, so you'll want to consult the book for more information, illustrations, and stories. At the beginning of each workbook session you'll see pointers to one or two chapters of the book. If you don't have the book, you can use this workbook on its own. However, you'll get much more out of this training series if you make time to read the book as well.

On the *Faith Path* companion DVD (sold separately) you'll find eight- to twelve-minute videos that go with each workbook session. When you meet with your group, you'll respond to a few questions, watch the video, and then discuss the rest of the session's questions. The DVD segments include some teaching from Mark as well as short interviews with some remarkable people talking about the faith paths they were on before they came to Christ.

You'll need a pen or pencil, because in most sessions you'll have some brief exercises to do on your own. These include short quizzes that will show you things about yourself that you may never have thought about before. They're fun, and you won't have to share your answers if you don't want to—though we think you'll want to!

Opening up and interacting with others in your group is the best way to get the most out of this workbook and your time together.

SESSION I

WHAT IS FAITH AND WHY DOES IT MATTER?

Everybody has faith. They may not be aware of it, but every person you know trusts in something that they can't prove or know in an absolute sense. And everybody has what we call a *faith path*, a way of deciding what to believe that leads them to their spiritual point of view. Many people don't realize they're living by faith, and few would be able to describe their faith path. But in this series we're going to talk about six common faith paths, and we'll see that some are definitely more helpful than others. Not all faith paths lead to something good. Some are dead ends.

In this first session, we'll explore the notion that everybody has faith. What does that mean? Is it true? And if it is true, how does it affect our lives? How does it impact our neighbor or coworker who doesn't believe in Christ but who may not have any idea he or she is living by faith in something or someone?

For more information on the material covered in this session, please read chapter 1 of *Choosing Your Faith.*

Before the DVD

1. Please take one minute to introduce yourself to the group and to complete the following sentence (if your group is larger than twelve people, tell a few people sitting near
   you):

   I chose the car I am currently driving because _____.

   *(Examples: Because I read a review that described how reliable it was.
   Because my friend had one, and she liked it. Because it looks cool.)*

What does choosing a car have to do with faith? Plenty!—as you'll see when you turn on
the DVD and hear from the author of this course, Mark Mittelberg.

Play DVD segment Session 1: What Is Faith and Why Does It Matter?

Write your notes from the DVD here:

After the DVD

If your group is larger than twelve people, gather into circles
of four or five people for this discussion.

---

2. What is one thing, person, or idea (a lemon of a car, a shady salesperson, a blind date,
   an attitude about money or work, etc.) that you trusted for the wrong reasons? (You
   don't have to tell the whole story—save it for after the group meeting.)

What is faith? It's not just mentally agreeing with a statement. It's not just believing something exists. Having faith in your car doesn't just mean believing it exists—it means trusting it enough to start up the engine and drive the car out on the road.

> *Faith is belief and action that are based on something we consider to be trustworthy, even though we don't have absolute proof.* That something might be an object, like your car; an idea, like democracy; or a person, like somebody you love or look up to, or the God who made you.

3. Are there any people you have faith in? Even a little bit? If so, who?

What are some actions you do that demonstrate that faith?

4. Are there any objects or ideas that you have faith in, even though you don't have absolute proof that they're true or reliable? If so, what are they?

What are some actions you do that demonstrate that faith?

Everybody has faith.

The serious Buddhist lives as if the eightfold path of Buddhism will lead to spiritual enlightenment. He can't prove that the tenets of his faith are sound, but he carries on in the hope that these are the right ideas that will lead to the best possible outcome.

Devout Muslims try to live by the five pillars of Islam, believing that Allah is God, Muhammad is his prophet, and the Quran is God's holy book. They can't know for certain that these things are true—there isn't a way to personally prove them—but they live by faith that they are right.

Committed Christians live in the trust that God exists and that Jesus is who he claimed to be—the unique Son of God. We believe that his death on the cross was allowed by God to atone for our sins, Jesus paying the spiritual death penalty in our place. We're convinced we have good reasons and evidence to conclude that these things are correct, and we stake our future as well as our present way of life on that trust. But it's trust just the same; we don't have absolute proof.

What about the casual Buddhist, Muslim, or Christian who merely pays lip service to their particular faith system but largely ignores it in daily life? There are millions of these people too—and they're living by faith that faith issues aren't very important to live by. Even the person who casually says, "Oh, I never worry about things like that!" lives by faith that people need not concern themselves about these matters.

This might surprise you, but even atheists live by faith. Why do I say that? Because they operate in the belief that there is no creator, no higher moral law to which they are accountable, no divine judgment, and no afterlife. They can't prove any of these things. They don't know for a fact that there is no God, spiritual standard, day of reckoning, or existence after death. In fact, most people in the world believe that denying these things goes against the evidence as well as human experience, and therefore requires *more* faith.

So everybody has faith—in something.[1]

5. On your own, make a list of three non-Christians whom you know (family members, friends, coworkers, mechanic, hairdresser—anybody you've talked to enough to have some sense of how they think).

Name:

Name:

Name:

6. Now, under each name above, write one idea you think that person has faith in as it relates to their spiritual life. For instance:

- Going out of my way to do good to others is what's most important.

- My main job in life is to look after myself and those close to me; I'll let God worry about the rest.

- People stress over too many things; the key to life is to relax and go with the flow. Everything always works out in the end.

- God helps those who help themselves.

- Following the teachings of my religion will lead to fulfillment.

- The one who ends up with the most toys wins.

- Pretty much everybody ends up in heaven—except the really bad people.

- I will be reincarnated on a higher level if I live a good life.

- I'm a good enough person to expect something good to happen to me after I die.

- There are no higher moral standards to which I'm accountable.

- There is no afterlife—life is like a candle; it finally flickers and just goes out.

Talk with your group about what you wrote. What did you learn? What similarities and differences do you notice?

7. Do you think the people you listed know why they believe what they do? What makes you think that?

How could you help them begin to think about their reasons—or perhaps their lack of reasons—for what they currently are trusting in?

You probably know that beliefs like this run deep, and badgering people to change their minds rarely works. So over the next few weeks, this training series will help you understand why your friends believe what they do. You'll learn about the faith paths they may have taken to get to their current beliefs, and you'll explore ways to help them examine their path and decide whether it's trustworthy enough to bet their lives on.

No matter what your friends believe, they still matter to God. Ultimately, he is the one who can lead someone to change their deepest beliefs. But you have an essential role to play, in partnership with the Holy Spirit, in your friends' lives. You may be one of the means God is using to draw your friends to him.

Prayer

If you're in a discussion group larger than eight people, subdivide into circles of four or five people for prayer. If you're not used to praying aloud in front of other people, it's okay to pray silently or to pray just one sentence. Nobody is keeping track, and there are no extra points for eloquence!

Pray for each other, asking God to use this training process to help you all know him better and to give you confidence and clarity as you interact with friends, neighbors, and family who don't yet know him. Ask him for a deeper love for the unbelievers in your life. And if there's anything else on your mind that you would like to talk to God about, share it with the others in your circle so they can pray with you.

I pray that your love will overflow more and more, and that you will keep on growing in knowledge and understanding. For I want you to understand what really matters, so that you may live pure and blameless lives until the day of Christ's return. (Philippians 1:9–10)

Coming up in session 2: How to relate to people who believe ideas like "You have your truth, and I have mine. Whatever works for you is good for you, but it's judgmental to say one way is right and someone else's way is wrong."

Reminder: Reading chapter 1 of *Choosing Your Faith* before we meet again will help you better understand the ideas we've covered in this session.

SESSION 2

TRUTH: A MATTER OF PERSPECTIVE?

THE PATH OF RELATIVISM

In the last session we learned that everybody has faith in something, even if they won't acknowledge it. We also discussed what some of our non-Christian friends currently are putting their trust in. As we move into this next session, our goal is, first, to begin to understand the various ways our friends have arrived at their beliefs—what we're calling the *six faith paths*—and, second, to learn how we can help them find the path toward the truth of Christ and his gospel message.

Maybe you've tried leading friends to Christ but felt like you were speaking a foreign language? Well, maybe you were! That different language isn't just Christian jargon like "Ya gotta get born again" and "You need to get into the Word" (both are biblical teachings, but unfortunately we sometimes trivialize them and turn them into easily misunderstood clichés). It's at a deeper level: the way people think, the way they're motivated. How does this or that person decide what they're going to believe? What drives them? Perhaps the appeal you made didn't appeal to them because they value and trust different factors than you do.

For example, many of us like to speak out of our experience. "I asked Jesus into my life," we say, "and he filled me with joy and peace—and he'll do the same for you!" But your friend isn't motivated by experience. He wants *reasons* to believe something is true. "How can you be sure it was Jesus that made you feel different?" he wonders aloud. "And how do you know that the Bible is reliable?" We may reply, "The Bible is the Word of God! It speaks with authority! Just read it and you'll see." But this person doesn't accept that because he doesn't trust subjective experiences like we're describing. He wants hard evidence.

Or we may face the opposite situation. Perhaps we've read a bunch of books like *The Case for Christ* and *Evidence That Demands a Verdict*, and we try to convey a mountain of logic and evidence to another friend, but she's not interested in our reasons. She says, "You can go on and on with all that academic stuff, but I know in my heart what is true. I don't need evidence because I have Oprah, and she and her spiritual teachers say we should look within ourselves and listen to our spirit. That's how I figure out what to believe."

You see, if we don't find out what the factors are that our friends rely on and somehow address those, then it really will be like we're speaking a different language. So for the next several sessions we're going to explore the various ways people decide what to believe. Once we know that, we'll be better able to point them to Christ.

In this session, we're going to look at the first of the six approaches—the one we refer to as the Relativistic faith path. This is the way more and more people in our culture choose their beliefs—especially young people who are influenced by secular schools and universities. We're going to learn how relativists think, and we'll evaluate the pros and cons of this way of approaching matters of faith.

For more information on the material covered in this session, please read chapter 2 of *Choosing Your Faith*.

Before the DVD

1. First, take two minutes to check in with someone sitting next to you. In *one sentence only*, tell them something about how your day has gone.

2. Next, before you turn on the DVD, take two minutes to do the following exercise on your own.

Read the statements below. To what degree does each one describe you or your beliefs? After reading each statement, write down the number that most closely reflects your response. Choose from 1 to 5, according to the following scale:

5 That's totally me.

4 That's usually like me.

3 That's a little like me.

2 That's barely like me.

1 That's not like me at all.

____ 1. What a person decides is true depends on his or her particular point of view.

____ 2. You shouldn't try to tell someone else what he or she ought to believe.

____ 3. Whatever you believe is true for you.

____ 4. What matters most is that you are sincere in your beliefs.

____ 5. Tolerance means acknowledging that everyone's ideas are true and valuable for them.

____ 6. It would be judgmental to say my way is right and someone else's is wrong.

____ 7. I can tell something is true by the fact that it's working in my life.

Now add up all seven numbers you wrote down, and write your total score here: _____

The quiz you've just taken gets at the degree to which the Relativistic mind-set appeals to you. You'll talk about your score after you view the DVD, but keep your responses in mind as you listen to Mark explain what relativism is, and as you hear a former relativist named Deb Bostwick talk about her experience on that faith path as the owner of a New Age bookstore. Listen for the things Deb believed as a relativist and for the things that started to disrupt her belief that she could create her own reality.

Play DVD segment Session 2: Relativism and Truth

Write your notes from the DVD here:

After the DVD

Before you viewed the DVD, you took a miniquiz of seven statements to see the degree to which you tend to live by a Relativistic mind-set. If your total score was 24 or higher, then you think like a relativist to some degree. Don't be embarrassed! Relativism has some significant problems, but it's an outlook that bombards us at school, on television, in films, from friends and perhaps family, and from the culture all around us. So it's no wonder many of us take these ideas for granted. On the plus side, if you're a relativist, you're probably a tolerant, nonjudgmental person who gets along with many kinds of people. But let's take a few minutes to evaluate some of the beliefs of relativism.

3. To what extent do you agree or disagree with the statement "It would be judgmental to say my way is right and someone else's is wrong"? Why?

4. What's the problem with the statement "Christianity is true for me, because I believe it—but maybe it's not true for you"?

5. What are some Christian beliefs that are either true for everybody or else not true at all?

We need to be clear on this: *Beliefs don't change reality.* If God really doesn't exist, then no matter how good our church experience is, and however much Christianity helps us feel better about ourselves, he's still a fantasy. On the other hand, if God *does* exist, then even though people may curse and deny him, they won't get rid of him. The real questions are "What's true about God?" and "How can we know?" Once we discover that, we should conform our beliefs accordingly.

Applying that principle, we'd say that Christianity is not true because we believe it, but rather, we believe it because we're convinced by the evidence that it is true! Furthermore, we should encourage our friends to join us in believing in things that prove to be trustworthy and true—and let go of beliefs that merely seem convenient or helpful.

Also, there's a big difference between saying you have a right to choose what you believe and saying you have the power to define reality. People should have the freedom to choose their own faith, without coercion—we believe in religious *tolerance*. But choosing to believe something doesn't make it actually *true*. We'll have to look to other faith paths—especially the sixth one—to answer the question of how we can determine what's really true.

6. What does a person have to give up in shifting from "My truth is what fits me" to "Truth is *what is,* whether I like it or not, whether it makes my life easier or more complicated"?

7. Why do you suppose relativism is such an appealing way of thinking today, even though there are such huge problems with it?

8. Do you know any relativists? Why do you think that's their faith path?

9. What are some of the challenges in talking to relativists about the Christian faith?

10. In the DVD, Mark uses the example of the truth about speed limits on the highway. How could you go about engaging a relativist in a conversation about this example?

11. If you were praying for a relativist, what would you ask God for?

Prayer

If you're in a discussion group larger than eight people, subdivide into circles of four or five people for prayer.

Don't copy the behavior and customs of this world, but let God trans-
form you into a new person by changing the way you think. Then you
will learn to know God's will for you, which is good and pleasing and
perfect. (Romans 12:2)

How can the others in your circle pray for you? Maybe you have a friend who tends to think like a relativist. How can the circle pray for you in that relationship? Can they ask God to help you grow in love for that person? Grow in understanding? Find ways of showing care for that person? Gain the courage to raise questions about truth with him or her?

Or maybe you have a tendency toward relativism, and perhaps you're not fully persuaded that it's a problem. Can the circle ask God to give you clarity and discernment?

Pray for each member of your circle.

Coming up in session 3: Many people simply accept the beliefs they were raised with as children and don't see any reason to question them. What's the potential downside of doing that?

Reminder: Reading chapter 2 of *Choosing Your Faith* before we meet again will help you better understand the ideas we've covered in this session.

SESSION 3

TESTING THE STATUS QUO

THE PATHS OF TRADITION AND AUTHORITY

Most families have traditions. Your family may have a special way it celebrates a particular holiday—or you may have a tradition of *not* celebrating certain holidays. You may have a custom of sitting down together each night to share a meal with silverware and fine china, or you may have a routine of eating take-out food on the run or "dining" in front of the television. We pick up all kinds of habits and hand-me-downs from our families in this way.

Families pass down faith traditions as well. Even a lack of belief in God can be a tradition passed down from parents to children. In this session we're going to look at the Traditional faith path—and its cousin, the Authoritarian faith path—to see their pros and cons and why and how they need to be tested.

For more information on the material covered in this session, please read chapters 3 and 4 of *Choosing Your Faith*.

Before the DVD

1. Share with someone sitting near you one tradition you had in your family growing
   up. *(Examples: The way you ate dinner together, or didn't eat together. A particular food
   you often had. What you did on a holiday. A television program you watched together.
   Something your parents believed, such as "God will always be there for you" or "You can't
   trust [some group or organization]," that they passed down to you.)*

2. Take a few minutes to do the following exercise on your own.

   Read the statements below. To what degree does each one describe you or your beliefs?
   After reading each statement, write down the number that most closely reflects your
   response. Choose from 1 to 5, according to the following scale:

   5 That's totally me.
   4 That's usually like me.
   3 That's a little like me.

2 That's barely like me.

1 That's not like me at all.

___ 1. I've never really thought about reasons for my faith. I just grew up believing it.

___ 2. It would be unwise to question what I've been taught within my faith tradition.

___ 3. My beliefs have been clear to me since I was taught them as a child.

___ 4. It makes sense to give deference to those in authority who have the ability and discernment needed to evaluate spiritual matters.

___ 5. I know by heart many of the words (of songs/Scriptures/readings/creeds) without necessarily knowing what they mean.

___ 6. It would be presumptuous to second-guess the teachings I've received; I don't have the training, knowledge, or formal degrees.

___ 7. I can hardly remember *not* going with my family to worship.

___ 8. If I don't follow what I'm taught, I will suffer the consequences.

___ 9. I don't think I could ever believe anything other than my religion; our family has practiced it for generations.

___ 10. I have a high degree of trust toward people whose talents, skills, and knowledge have brought them to spiritual leadership.

___ 11. I go to meetings at the church/mosque/temple/synagogue/group because that's our custom—it's just what we do.

___ 12. Our book says it, and I believe it.

___ 13. It's hard for me to think about *not* being involved in my particular faith; it's part of my whole heritage and identity.

___ 14. It's a high value in my religion to humbly submit to what the leaders say.

Now add up all seven numbers you wrote for the *odd-numbered* items, and write your total score for the Traditional path. Then add up the numbers you wrote for the *even-numbered* items, and write your total score for the Authoritarian path.

Traditional path (odd-numbered items): _____

Authoritarian path (even-numbered items): _____

You'll talk about your score in this quiz after you view the DVD, but keep your responses in mind as you listen to Mark explain these two paths and as you hear two people talk about their experiences on these paths. Jennifer Dion will talk about growing up in a family that took Christian teachings and traditions for granted and didn't encourage her to ask questions or to discuss her doubts as a teenager. Then Nabeel Qureshi, who is now a leader of Acts 17 Apologetics (www.Acts17.net), will recount how authority figures and an unquestioned authoritative book influenced his life as a Muslim.

Play DVD segment Session 3: Testing the Status Quo—The Paths of Tradition and Authority

Write your notes from the DVD here:

After the DVD

Before you viewed the DVD, you took a miniquiz of fourteen statements to see the degree to which you tend to live by the Traditional or Authoritarian faith path. If your total score was 24 or higher for either, then you tend to live by that path to at least some degree. (Feel free to share your scores with others in the group if you'd like to.)

Tradition and authority have important roles in the Christian community. Some traditions carry forward the truth from generation to generation, including those instituted by Jesus, like the Lord's Supper. Some authorities speak for truth and lead for good. Trusting them without question can be easy for some of us, and mistrusting them without reason may be easy for others of us—but neither choice is wise. Instead, we need to learn how to evaluate traditions and authorities in order to keep what is good and let go of what is not.

Let's start by discussing the Traditional faith path.

3. What are some good things we can get from tradition? (Perhaps mention some examples of positive things you've gained.)

Read aloud Mark 7:5–8:

> *So the Pharisees and teachers of religious law asked him, "Why don't your disciples follow our age-old tradition? They eat without first performing the hand-washing ceremony."*
>
> *Jesus replied, "You hypocrites! Isaiah was right when he prophesied about you, for he wrote,*
>
> *'These people honor me with their lips,*
> *   but their hearts are far from me.*
> *Their worship is a farce,*
> *   for they teach man-made ideas as commands from God.'*
>
> *For you ignore God's law and substitute your own tradition."*

4. What flaws does Jesus criticize in that passage related to blindly following tradition?

5. Is it possible to practice Christian traditions, or the Christian faith we grew up with in general, without falling into these errors? If so, how? If not, why not?

6. Now let's think about the Authoritarian faith path. Based on what we heard in the video, how is the Authoritarian faith path like the Traditional one, and how are they different?

7. Are there any religious authorities you think are at least generally reliable? If so, who are they, and what gives you that confidence?

As we heard, it's not a question of *if* we'll be under authority. We need doctors and teachers and coaches and police officers and people to run the government and people to help us know God. The question is *which* authorities we'll trust and respond to.

It's essential to ask, *What are the credentials of this authority figure?* If we're looking for medical advice, is this a doctor with good medical credentials? If we're looking for the truth about God, what are the credentials of this teacher?

Also, it's good to have checks and balances and "second opinions." An opinion from a second doctor can protect us from the errors or oversights of the first doctor. One branch of government helps keep an eye on another branch. The same is often true in the spiritual realm. The practical challenge for us and for our friends, as it relates to choosing our faith, is to muster up the courage and the clarity to reconsider and test the credentials of the spiritual authorities in our lives. These may be people or organizations that are already in leadership roles over us, or those that would like to be. We need to scrutinize what they say, teach, and do, and then compare and contrast them to other spiritual authorities that have proven to be reliable, always looking to see whether they exhibit the marks of truthfulness, character, and spiritual authenticity.

Here are four key characteristics we can encourage our friends to look for in order to tell whether an authority figure, an organization, the founder of a religion, the writings of a religion, or the leaders of a religion have good credentials:

- *Integrity.* Does the leader live with (not just talk about) love, honesty, integrity, and humility? (Jesus did. Modern church leaders should—and if they don't, we understand why non-Christians don't trust them. If you have a Mormon or Muslim friend, do some research on how Joseph Smith or Muhammad lived, especially compared to Jesus.)

- *Consistency.* Does the leader live that way over the long haul, and when they fail, do they humbly acknowledge their mistakes, make necessary changes, implement safeguards and accountability, and move forward with greater faithfulness? (Everybody except Jesus has flaws, and your pastor is no different. The crucial thing to pay attention to is the way a leader deals with his or her failings. Look for humility and, with it, the willingness to learn and grow in godliness. Untrustworthy religious leaders tend to make excuses for their behavior, sometimes even justifying it as divinely allowed for them.)

- *Accuracy.* Is the leader or organization's teaching (1) true to the world, (2) true to the leader's own words, and (3) true to God's words? True to the world means that if they teach something about the physical world, it's accurate. By contrast, the Book of Mormon makes claims about whole ancient civilizations about which archaeologists can find no evidence. True to the leader's own words means, for instance, that if a healing ministry proclaims that a person "has been healed from polio," that person needs to have had the symptoms in the first place and then be truly free of those symptoms tonight, tomorrow, and six months from now. Or, if a self-proclaimed prophet predicts something in the name of the Lord, it needs to happen. True to God's words points toward the Bible as a standard for measuring other authorities—we'll deal with why that is valid in session 7.

- *Openness.* Is this leader or organization fully open to having their integrity, consistency, and accuracy scrutinized and tested? Or are they secretive or defensive?

Do they take offense if you ask questions about the current leadership's actions or the actions of the group's original founder?

(For more on these four characteristics, see chapter 4 of *Choosing Your Faith*.)
It's wise to pray and ask God to show you whether a particular leader or religious organization has integrity, consistency, accuracy, and openness. Also, go ahead and scrutinize Jesus as he is portrayed in the Bible, and scrutinize the Bible, too. (We'll explore how to do that in session 7.) As you probably know, they pass the tests with flying colors!

8. Do you know anyone who's on the Traditional or Authoritarian faith path? If so, what makes you think that's their path?

9. What are some reasons why a person might resist investigating whether their traditional beliefs are true or their authorities are trustworthy?

10. How can we help a person like this understand the value of investigating their beliefs and teachers or leaders?

11. How would you pray for a person on a Traditional or Authoritarian faith path who doesn't know Christ?

Prayer

If you're in a discussion group larger than eight people, subdivide into circles of four or five people for prayer.

Show me the right path, O LORD;

point out the road for me to follow.

Lead me by your truth and teach me,

for you are the God who saves me.

All day long I put my hope in you. (Psalm 25:4–5)

Share with the others in your circle the first name of one person you know who is on a Traditional or Authoritarian path. How can the circle pray for you in that relationship or for that person directly? Can they ask God to show you how to help that person examine his or her beliefs? Or should they pray for trust to first grow in that relationship?

Or maybe you've been on a Traditional or Authoritarian faith path yourself. If so, how can the group pray for you concerning your own process of testing and confirming your faith?

Pray for each member of your circle.

Coming up in session 4: Lots of people think that in spiritual matters it's wiser to trust your heart or instincts than logic and evidence. What are the pros and cons of trusting your heart? And how can we communicate with non-Christians who take this approach?

Reminder: Reading chapters 3 and 4 of *Choosing Your Faith* before we meet again will help you better understand the ideas we've covered in this session.

Session 4

Evaluating Feelings and Experience

The Intuitive and Mystical Paths

Our society places a high value on personal experience. We don't just want a cup of coffee; we want the full Starbucks experience. Many of us enjoy video games and movies that provide ever-increasing levels of adrenaline-packed immersion into virtual realities. In such a culture, religion that addresses people largely from the neck up is considered out of vogue. Instead, many people flock to spiritualities that appeal to them from the neck down—low on doctrine and high on emotion and intuitive or mystical experience. In this session we'll take a look at some of those forms of spirituality and consider how to talk about matters of faith with people who are drawn to them. We'll also explore what place intuition and mystical experience have in Christian faith.

For more information on the material covered in this session, please read chapters 5 and 6 of *Choosing Your Faith*.

Before the DVD

1. Share with someone sitting near you two or three words that describe aspects of your personality. *(For example: shy, outgoing, logical, emotional, spontaneous, careful.)*

2. Take a few minutes to do the following exercise on your own.

   As we've done before, read the statements below. To what degree does each one describe you or your beliefs? After reading each statement, write down the number that most closely reflects your response. Choose from 1 to 5, according to the following scale:

   5   That's totally me.
   4   That's usually like me.
   3   That's a little like me.
   2   That's barely like me.
   1   That's not like me at all.

___ 1. Your senses can deceive you; you're better off listening to your heart.

___ 2. I have confidence in what I believe because God showed me it's true.

___ 3. I can just feel what is right or true.

___ 4. It may have been through a dream, a vision, or an apparition, but one way or another I got "the message," and I follow it today.

___ 5. My friends and I talk about spiritual things and then just decide what to believe.

___ 6. I know my spiritual direction is right because I often sense God's presence.

___ 7. I know what the so-called spiritual experts try to tell us, but I have a hunch they're often wrong.

___ 8. You can study your books and consult the experts, but God told me what's right, and for me that settles it.

___ 9. I can usually tell within seconds if something is true.

___ 10. When our group gets together to study or worship, we can literally feel God's presence, and that gives us confidence our beliefs are on the right track.

___ 11. Generally, my mistakes have come when I've ignored my inner voice or "gut feelings."

___ 12. Whether it was an angel or some other kind of spiritual personage, I can't ignore the insights my experiences have given me.

___ 13. I think many people have what might be called a "sixth sense" about what is right and true, and they need to follow it.

___ 14. I didn't know what to think, so I prayed and asked for supernatural guidance, and I was given direction about which way I should go.

Now add up all seven numbers you wrote for the *odd-numbered* items, and write your total score for the Intuitive path. Then add up the numbers you wrote for the *even-numbered* items, and write your total score for the Mystical path.

Intuitive path (odd-numbered items): _____

Mystical path (even-numbered items): _____

We'll look at what your scores mean in a few moments, but first let's watch a video in which Mark will discuss these two faith paths and explain their differences. We'll also hear from Vipool Patel, president of www.JesusCentral.com, talking about his experience on the Intuitive faith path, and Elle Karp regarding her journey as a Mormon on the Mystical path.

Play DVD segment Session 4: Evaluating Feelings and Experience— The Intuitive and Mystical Paths

Write your notes from the DVD here:

After the DVD

Before you viewed the DVD, you took a miniquiz of fourteen statements to see the degree to which you tend to live by the Intuitive or Mystical path. If your total score was 24 or higher for either faith path, then you tend to live by that path to at least some degree. (Feel free to share your scores with others in the group.)

Like tradition and authority, intuition and mystical experiences can have important roles in the Christian community. Some of us are more engaged in these areas than others, and that can lead us to either overvalue or undervalue what they contribute. But rather than accepting them uncritically or immediately viewing them with suspicion, we need to test them with evidence and logic. Far from being opposed to reason, intuition works best in partnership with reason.

3. What are some ways intuition can work for Christians?

4. Do you agree with Mark's critique of spiritual movements that tell us to trust our hearts but not our senses? Why or why not?

Beyond simple intuitive awareness, which can be very helpful, the Intuitive faith path can treat head and heart as opposing forces. According to this approach, real perception resides in feelings and instinct, and doctrine is often considered unimportant or even undesirable. The heart gives the most reliable sense of direction. That direction will often be gained in hidden places and be overlooked by the masses of people—who are caught up in the world of sights and sounds and who are missing the deeper realities only available to those who search them out using their innate sixth sense.

One factor that makes this path appealing is its intrigue. The idea of knowing things others don't know through internal and hidden processes has a certain mystique. It also seems to sidestep the need for rigorous thought, study, investigation, and accountability. Another appeal can be the idea that if you properly focus your mental energy, it will bring great rewards—success in romance, business, or finances.

5. What's wrong with following a path like this that sidesteps rigorous thought yet promises rewards like success in romance, business, or finances?

6. Do you know anybody who seems to form his or her spiritual views through the Intuitive faith path? If so, describe some of what he or she believes and practices.

Intuition can be the flashing yellow light that signals danger or opportunity. Most of the time, the best way to respond is to say, "Here's what my intuition is telling me; now what other information reinforces or contradicts it?" Sometimes there isn't perfect evidence either way, and we have to make a decision, but that's very different from saying, "Logic and evidence are pointing one way, but I'm going the opposite way because I have this feeling." Or, "I'm not going to bother seeking more information because I know my intuition is right."

The same is true of mystical encounters. The Bible and Christian history are full of mystical encounters between humans and God or angels. We should be open to them, but we also have to test them.

The apostle Paul had more than one mystical experience (Acts 26:9–25; 2 Corinthians 12:1–10). With a keen sense of balance, he wrote, "Do not put out the Spirit's fire; do not treat prophecies with contempt. Test everything. Hold on to the good. Avoid every kind of evil" (1 Thessalonians 5:19–22 NIV). The great Christian mystics have always emphasized their need for a keen understanding of biblical doctrine in order to separate trustworthy experiences from deceptive ones.

In chapter 6 of *Choosing Your Faith*, Mark presents two formulas to help us evaluate mystical encounters. Here's the first one, which says that our feelings do not necessarily equate to something real:

$$\text{Feel} \neq \text{Real}$$

7. What is an example (maybe from the video or your own experience) of feeling something that wasn't real?

Expectations within a religious culture can cause people to have feelings (such as a "burning in the soul") that they've been told they should feel. Music can stir intense emotions, as can passionate teaching, the beauty of nature, or hearing other people tell emotional stories about their experiences. Even sheer exhaustion can trigger feelings that mimic spirituality but have nothing to do with the real spiritual world. It's normal to be awed by a magnificent mountain or moved by intense music, but these feelings on their own don't validate any given set of beliefs. And if a secular person sits down for the first time in her life to read a widely known religious book, with the promise that something is bound to happen, and for the first time prays to something greater than herself, it's easy to imagine that positive emotions might arise. But those emotions don't necessarily mean that the book (the Book of Mormon, for example) records the truth or is from God.

Here's the second formula, which tells us something can be real but not necessarily good or from God:

Real ≠ Good

The Bible tells us that there are real spiritual forces other than God, opposed to God, and they actively try to deceive people.

8. What is an example of a real mystical experience that isn't good—whether in the Bible or experience? *(Optional: Check out the very strange story in 1 Samuel 28:3–25.)*

9. Think of someone you know who places a lot of value on intuitive or mystical experiences. If you explained these two statements (Feel ≠ Real and Real ≠ Good), do you think your friend would agree, or do you think they'd argue with one or both statements? Why?

Intuitives and mystics tend to place great trust in personal experience, so one way to begin a conversation with them is to talk first about your own experience with God. You could also tell them about the testimonies you heard in this session's DVD segment. Or you might want to connect your intuitive or mystical friend with someone in your group who has had intuitive or mystical experiences but sorted out which parts were from God and were therefore trustworthy.

10. Have you ever had a powerful experience that felt real but wasn't or that was real but not ultimately good? Have you ever followed your heart and ignored your head? If so, tell your group a little about that experience if you feel comfortable doing so.

11. Have you ever had an intuitive or mystical experience you believe was both real and good? If so, briefly share that story with your group if you feel comfortable doing so, and talk about how you could use your experiences to talk to friends.

Another way of starting a conversation with your friends on any of the faith paths is to give them copies of the book *Choosing Your Faith*. You can share with them your experience of being in this group and tell them why you think they might enjoy the book. Rather than sending the message that you want to change or "fix" them, you can simply say that you personally have gotten something out of the group and want to share it.

If you are intuitive or mystical yourself, you may benefit in particular from the guidance in chapters 5 and 6 about how to make sure an intuition or mystical encounter is true to the world, true to the messenger's own words, and true to God's words.

12. How could you best pray for a friend on an Intuitive or Mystical faith path who doesn't know Christ?

Prayer

If you're in a discussion group larger than eight people, subdivide into circles of four or five people for prayer.

I pray for you constantly, asking God, the glorious Father of our Lord Jesus Christ, to give you spiritual wisdom and insight so that you might grow in your knowledge of God. I pray that your hearts will be flooded with light so that you can understand the confident hope he has given to those he called—his holy people who are his rich and glorious inheritance. (Ephesians 1:16–18)

How can the group pray for you? Maybe you know someone who is on the Intuitive or Mystical path, and you'd like wisdom and insight concerning how to share Christ with that person. Or maybe you're an intuitive or mystical person yourself, and you need God's help to discern what's really from him.

Pray for each member of your circle.

Coming up in session 5: How logic and evidence can help us and our non-Christian friends avoid spiritual pitfalls.

Reminder: Reading chapters 5 and 6 of *Choosing Your Faith* before we meet again will help you better understand the ideas we've covered in this session.

SESSION 5

GETTING AT THE TRUTH

THE POWER OF THE EVIDENTIAL PATH

We've looked at five faith paths so far. Most of them can provide at least potential contributions in leading a person toward truth, but none of them is adequate on its own. All of them need to be tested by a sixth approach, the one we'll explore in this session: the Evidential faith path.

For more information on the material covered in this session, please read chapters 7 and 8 of *Choosing Your Faith*.

Before the DVD

1. Turn to someone sitting near you and complete this sentence: "To me, logic is _____."

2. Take a couple of minutes to do the following exercise on your own.

Read the statements below. To what degree does each one describe you or your beliefs? After reading each statement, write down the number that most closely reflects your response. Choose from 1 to 5, according to the following scale:

> 5 That's totally me.
> 4 That's usually like me.
> 3 That's a little like me.
> 2 That's barely like me.
> 1 That's not like me at all.

____ 1. Spiritual teachings need to add up logically; I don't have to fully understand them, but I can't believe anything that's self-contradictory.

____ 2. People have all kinds of hunches and instincts; if they're not careful, those can get them into a lot of trouble.

____ 3. I think we should just deal with the facts; it's okay if they challenge conventional thinking.

____ 4. I'd like to believe things people tell me, but I've got to check them out first.

____ 5. It's easy to glamorize "following your heart" or hanging on to ancient traditions, but the question is whether or not a claim is actually true.

____ 6. It's hard to argue with the evidence.

____ 7. I just try to weigh the information I'm given, carefully consider the source, and reach a logical conclusion.

Now add up all seven numbers you wrote down, and write your total score here: _____

Before we get to the details of what this means, let's watch a video of Lee Strobel talking about his experiences on the Evidential faith path, and Mark teaching about why this approach is so important to us, and to our friends. (Lee Strobel is a best-selling author and popular speaker, and his Web site features hundreds of videos on questions about Christianity: www.LeeStrobel.com.)

Play DVD segment Session 5: Getting at the Truth—The Power of the Evidential Path

Write your notes from the DVD here:

After the DVD

Before you viewed the DVD, you took a miniquiz of seven statements to see the degree to which you utilize the Evidential faith path. If your total score was 24 or higher, then this is probably your favored path.

3. In what ways are you like Lee, who spoke in the DVD?

In what ways are you different?

4. Mark explained some of the reasons for using logic and evidence to test beliefs. What did you find persuasive or unpersuasive?

If you're more naturally drawn to one of the other faith paths, how do you respond to the idea of testing your intuition, tradition, etc. with evidence?

The Law of Non-Contradiction

The law of non-contradiction asserts that two conflicting statements can't both be true. For example, consider these two statements:

- My car's gas tank is empty.

- My car's gas tank contains gasoline.

These two statements can't both be true at the same time. Even a relativist or a Zen Buddhist will not operate his car as if the emptiness or non-emptiness of his gas tank is unknowable or meaningless. He will not say, "Here, let me drive, because for you the tank may be empty, but for me it contains gas." (If he *does* say that, he'll probably call you later—asking for a ride!)

5. Imagine you have a friend who says Christianity, Judaism, and Islam are all true. How could you talk to such a friend about the following beliefs of these three religions?

- *Christian beliefs:* Jesus of Nazareth is the Jewish Messiah and the Savior of the world foretold in the Hebrew Bible (Old Testament). The New Testament presents true information about him: He was the Son of God, he died on a cross to pay for our sins, and he rose from the dead.

- *Jewish beliefs:* The Messiah who was foretold in the Hebrew Bible has not yet come, but we should pray for his coming. Jesus was not the Messiah, he was not a true prophet, he died on the cross, but he did not rise from the dead.

- *Islamic beliefs:* Jesus was a true prophet of God, but he was not the Son of God and never claimed to be, he did not die on the cross, and he did not rise from the dead.

6. What if your friend says it's *not important* to nail down which, if any, of these statements about Jesus are true, as long as we all respect each other and get along peacefully? How could you logically show why the truth of these statements matters?

On the other hand, what if your friend doubts that it's *possible* to know what's true about Jesus, who lived twenty centuries ago? Then it's time to talk about evidence. In sessions 6 and 7, you will learn some of the evidence that points toward the Bible's claims, and you will address the question of whether there's adequate historical information to decide about Jesus.

For some of us, learning and explaining the evidence for the New Testament's claims seems overwhelming. If we were good at gathering and presenting evidence, we'd be lawyers or scientists! But it doesn't have to be that hard. At the end of session 7, you'll also find a list of books that do a great job of collecting the evidence and making it understandable. In addition, chapters 9–11 of *Choosing Your Faith* summarize twenty key areas of evidence in ways that are easy to grasp and share with others.

The Arbitrary Limiting of Evidence

Logic and sensory experience are essential tools in deciding which beliefs are worth embracing. And, as those who love truth, we should be open to following the evidence and information wherever they lead us. This is a big part of what gives us confidence as Christians—knowing that our faith is built upon facts.

But some people apply logic and experience in ways that color their conclusions. In the last couple of centuries, some thinkers have hijacked genuine science and transformed it into an ideology sometimes called *scientism* (though most of those who operate with this mind-set would not refer to it with this term). Scientism is "the belief that the scientific method is the only method for discovering truth."[1] Scientism determines in advance what kinds of conclusions will be considered acceptable. Supernatural causes are automatically ruled out, even if strong historical or physical evidence points toward them. All scientific research—including research on questions like how the universe began or what makes humans unique—must be done as if atheism were an established fact that cannot be questioned.

Scientism also rules out a God who acts within history. Therefore, there was no creation of a universe out of nothing, and there are no virgin births, no miracles of any kind, and certainly no resurrections from the dead—these things are not disproved, but simply placed outside the limits of consideration.

One of the logical flaws here is that the scientific method is unable to prove that it is the only method for discovering truth—that is just taken as a rule or assumption up front. In other words, *scientism can't be proven scientifically!* And it is certainly unable to prove that supernatural forces or beings do not exist.

We need to encourage our friends who think along these lines not to arbitrarily limit the full range of possible explanations for things they see in the world and in the realm of the seemingly supernatural. A truly open-minded person would at least consider the possibility that something appearing to be supernatural might actually *be* supernatural.

7. Do you know anybody who believes in what we've described as scientism? What makes you associate him or her with this belief system?

8. What are some things you might say to challenge the thinking of a person like this?

9. How would you pray for a friend who is trusting something based on one of the other faith paths—even though it goes against logic or evidence?

Prayer

If you're in a discussion group larger than eight people, subdivide into circles of four or five people for prayer.

---

*We use God's mighty weapons, not worldly weapons, to knock down
the strongholds of human reasoning and to destroy false arguments.
We destroy every proud obstacle that keeps people from knowing God.
We capture their rebellious thoughts and teach them to obey Christ.
(2 Corinthians 10:4–5)*

How can the others in your circle pray for you? Maybe you have a relationship with someone who is vehement about scientism, and you find those interactions challenging. Or maybe applying logic to religious beliefs or wielding evidence feels unnatural to you. Do you need wisdom or courage or deeper love—or maybe just a block of time in which to think things through?

Pray for the members of your circle.

Coming up in session 6: Now that you see the value of evidence, we'll take a look at some solid reasons for believing that God exists.

Reminder: Reading chapters 7 and 8 of *Choosing Your Faith* before we meet again will help you better understand the ideas we've covered in this session.

Session 6

Elements of a Confident Faith, Part 1

Arrows of Truth

We've now looked at six faith paths, six different ways people decide what to believe and trust, especially in the spiritual realm. While most of these approaches can contribute vital information and inspiration for our spiritual journeys, we've given the most weight to the sixth one, the one that focuses on evidence. Why? Mark will talk about that in a moment.

Before the DVD

1. Think of one person you've interacted with in the past couple of days. Turn to someone sitting near you now and tell them:

    • Which faith path do you think the person you've thought of prefers to use in choosing what he or she believes? (The six paths are Relativistic, Traditional, Authoritarian, Intuitive, Mystical, and Evidential.)

    • What is one reason why you think that's this person's preferred path?

    If you can't remember the ins and outs of all the paths, don't worry. We'll review them in this session, and you can go back through your workbook later. As you watch the DVD, please think about this question: *How does the Evidential path help us test what we learn from each of the other paths?*

 Play DVD segment Session 6: Elements of a Confident Faith, Part 1—Arrows of Truth

Write your notes from the DVD here:

After the DVD

2. Imagine that you know five people who are following a different one of the five paths listed below. How would you explain to them the value of using logic and evidence to evaluate what they've learned through their path?

The Relativistic path

The Traditional path

The Authoritarian path

The Intuitive path

The Mystical path

By now you may be thinking, *Okay, what is this evidence that can help people on these various paths begin to test what they believe? What's the evidence that supports the teachings of the Bible and Christianity?* For the rest of this session and in session 7, we're going to take a very summarized look at a number of reasons and arguments that support our faith. We'll call these arguments "Arrows of Truth."

We won't go through all twenty Arrows of Truth listed in *Choosing Your Faith*, but you can find them all explained in chapters 9–11. The arrows we'll discuss in this session are selected and adapted from chapter 9.

3. Below are short summaries of four arguments for the belief that an astonishingly intelligent, wise, and powerful Creator exists. Take a few minutes on your own to read these four arguments (the arrow numbers correspond to the numbers in the *Choosing Your Faith* book—and since we won't study all of the arguments presented there, you'll notice some numbering gaps).

Arrow 1: Design in the universe points to an Intelligent Designer. If you find a watch on the ground, you immediately realize it's not a fluke of nature or a product of mere chance. Watches, because of their complexity and design, require a watchmaker. Whenever something shows evidence of having been made for a purpose, it points us back to a cause behind it, an intelligence that designed it. A single living cell is immensely complex—far beyond any watch—and adapted to its function in a way that strongly suggests design. Even a functional protein or gene is far too complex for us to create in a laboratory, and those are just some of the building blocks of a cell. It would take an immense leap of faith to believe these complexities, and those of every form of life on the planet, developed independently by blind chance! Rather, the evidence seems to point clearly to an Intelligent Designer.

Arrow 2: Fine-tuning in the universe points to an intentional Fine Tuner. Our growing understanding of "constants" in physics points to the astonishing degree of fine-tuning the universe needed in order to support life. For instance, scientists tell us that the energy density of empty space has to be just right. The precision of this constant has to be one in 10^{73} (that's 10 with 73 zeroes after it). That's like shooting an arrow from out in space and hitting the bull's-eye of a target in Texas. And if the odds are that small of the universe just happening to have this energy density by chance, how small are they if we add another thirty or so factors just as tightly constrained? Are there an infinite number of universes out there that have formed by chance, and we just happen to be in the one in a zillion that can sustain life? That's a story some scientists like to tell, but it lacks evidence. It seems much more likely, and in light of the amazing examples of fine-tuning it takes much less faith, to simply acknowledge that the universe was fine-tuned by a divine Fine Tuner!

Arrow 3: Information encoded into DNA points to a Divine Encoder. Each cell of the human body carries DNA. DNA is a coded text that tells the cell (and ultimately the body) what to do. According to Francis Collins, former head of the Human Genome Project, which mapped the human DNA sequence, DNA's coded text is "3 billion letters long, and written in a strange and cryptographic four-letter code."[1] Is it credible to believe that information this complex came to be recorded and communicated by chance? If you saw something even as simple as the words *John loves Mary* written on the beach, would you entertain the possibility that the waves might have formed them by chance? Or would you surmise that an intelligent communicator wrote them? How much more does the DNA code point to an intelligent Divine Encoder?

Arrow 5: The sense of morality throughout the human race points to a Moral Lawgiver. Everybody has an internal standard of morality—but one that is above us and comes from outside of us. Why *above* and *outside*? Because everybody has it, but nobody consistently lives up to it. Why would we each invent a code of ethics that we could never quite fulfill and then employ it to frustrate and condemn ourselves all life long? We may disagree about a few particular moral issues, but people in every culture agree that the Adolf Hitlers among us are evil or crazy or both—because virtually everyone knows that committing murder is wrong, including those who do it. Where does this moral sense come from? Did it evolve through some kind of "survival of the fittest" instincts? That's doubtful, since those instincts would lead us to do whatever we had to do to survive, including committing some of the acts that our moral sense tells us are wrong! Rather, our innate sense of morality points powerfully to the existence of a Moral Lawgiver—one who wove his standards into the very fabric of what it means to be human.

4. Now, as a group, discuss each of the above arguments (arrows) in turn. About each one, ask yourselves:

- Do I understand this argument? If not, can others in the group help make it clearer? Or do I need more information, such as the longer explanations in *Choosing Your Faith*?

- Do I find this argument convincing? If not, why not?

- Does this sort of argument matter to me personally? Why or why not?

- Do I know any non-Christians who might find it helpful to think about this information? If so, who? Do I feel equipped to talk about it, or might I want to give my friend *Choosing Your Faith* or one of the resource books recommended at the end of session 7?

5. At the end of this discussion, take a few minutes on your own to write down anything you want to do as a result of this discussion. For instance, you might write the name

of a non-Christian friend or acquaintance and make a note to yourself about some evidence (or a book) that might interest him or her.

You can probably tell from your discussion that not every non-Christian—or even every Christian—is equally receptive to this kind of evidence. Those on the Relativistic path may say this is useful for you but not for them. Someone on an Intuitive path might dismiss this as head information rather than heart perception. So we can't just present this evidence to such people and expect it to bear fruit. Instead, we need to interact with them about how they think, what motivates them, and whether their current path is really reliable as a sole source of spiritual information and guidance. Once they begin to see the value of logic and evidence, then we can provide them with strong examples of it.

Prayer

If you're in a discussion group larger than eight people, subdivide into circles of four or five people for prayer.

The heavens proclaim the glory of God.

The skies display his craftsmanship.

Day after day they continue to speak;

night after night they make him known. (Psalm 19:1–2)

How can the others in your circle pray for you? Maybe you have a relationship with someone who would benefit from evidence that points to God's existence, but you're nervous about bringing up the subject. Maybe you have a friend who seems closed to information of this kind and you don't know how to help that person see its value.

Pray for each member of your circle.

Coming up in session 7: What can you say to someone who says that the Bible is just a book of myths or that the notion of Jesus being the Son of God is ridiculous? You don't have to tell them these are just "your truths" or that "God says so." There are solid, objective reasons you can give to show the reliability of the Bible and its claims about Jesus.

Reminder: Reading chapter 9 of *Choosing Your Faith* before we meet again will help you better understand the ideas we've covered in this session.

Session 7

Elements of a Confident Faith, Part 2

More Arrows of Truth

In session 6, we looked at scientific evidence that points to the existence of a wise and powerful God. That's evidence for *a* God, but not necessarily *the* God revealed in the Bible and in Jesus Christ. So in this session we're going to take that next step. We'll look at evidence that shows the Bible is reliable (especially as compared to the foundational texts of other religions). We'll also look at historical evidence for believing what the New Testament says about Jesus.

We won't go through all of the remaining Arrows of Truth in detail, but you can find them explained in chapters 10 and 11 of *Choosing Your Faith*. The arrows discussed in this session are selected and adapted from those chapters.

Before the DVD

1. Think of a non-Christian you've observed this week, either someone you've encountered in person, or someone you've seen on television or elsewhere in the media. Which faith path do you think that person is on, and why? Share your answer with one person sitting near you.

The DVD for this session is divided into two segments: a very short one that you should view now and a longer one that you'll view toward the end of your meeting.

 Play DVD segment 1 of Session 7: Elements of a Confident Faith, Part 2—More Arrows of Truth

Write your notes from the DVD here:

After the DVD

Gather in your smaller discussion circles for this part of your meeting.

Below are summaries for eight more arrows that point toward the truth of the Christian faith. You may not have time to deal with all eight of them, so give everyone a few minutes of silence to look over the arrows on their own and choose one or two that seem intriguing to them or, better yet, useful in talking to their friends. Remember that these are very short summaries that are explained more fully in *Choosing Your Faith*.

First, here are four arrows pointing to the reliability of the Bible:

Arrow 7: The Bible is a uniquely historical religious book. The New Testament accounts are based mostly on direct eyewitness testimonies. They are compiled either by the eyewitnesses themselves or by writers who talked with the eyewitnesses (see, for example, Luke 1:1–4). And contrary to what you may have heard, all of the New Testament books were written within the life span of people who had known Jesus and could vouch for the accuracy of what was written. Most of the books were written within forty years, and all of them within about sixty years, after Jesus' resurrection. By comparison, the revised account of Jesus in the Islamic text, the Quran, was written some six hundred years later and was based on what was claimed to be a message from an angel. And the Book of Mormon is based on golden tablets that Joseph Smith allegedly dug up in New York State in the nineteenth century. He said that he translated the tablets into English before an angel whisked them away. The historical nature of the Bible stands out in sharp contrast to these other religious writings.

Arrow 8: The Bible is a uniquely preserved work of antiquity. Every good English translation we have today is based on early manuscripts in the original languages, Hebrew for the Old Testament and Greek for the New Testament. For the New Testament we have thousands of early Greek (full or partial) manuscripts. There are far more copies of the New Testament books than of any other ancient work, such as Homer's *Iliad* or the writings of Plato. Our earliest Greek New Testament manuscripts are copies that can be dated to within a generation of the originals (compared to a thousand years after the original for the *Iliad*). And because we have thousands of early copies or fragments of the New Testament books (compared to only seven copies of Plato), we can compare the copies and show that the variations among them are mostly insignificant—a miscopied word or phrase—and none of the variations affect any important teachings or doctrines. No other work from the ancient world has been preserved with the kind of care and accuracy that the Bible has—not even close.

Arrow 10: The Bible shows itself to be a uniquely honest religious book. Some people have said that Christianity is all about wish fulfillment—that people wanted a religion to make them feel better, so they projected a heavenly Father into the sky and added additional comforting myths. The problem with this theory is that the Bible contains a lot of sobering information that is the opposite of what people would make up if they were inventing a comforting religion. The God of the Bible sometimes punishes the disobedience of people, sometimes even his friends, in ways that can seem abrupt and harsh. The Bible warns of dire eternal consequences for living to suit one's sinful pleasures. It claims that we all have corrupted hearts that lead us into all kinds of moral trouble and turn us into spiritually bankrupt people who desperately need to be rescued. Nobody would have invented these realities to make themselves feel better. The Bible is also brutally honest about the ethical and moral failures of some of its key characters, including even some of its own writers. These negative but realistic elements are signs that the Bible is a trustworthy record that has not been sanitized by later editors.

Arrow 12: Fulfilled prophecies point to the Bible as a divinely inspired book and to Jesus as the unique Messiah of God. Here is a well-known Bible verse: "All of us, like sheep, have strayed away. We have left God's paths to follow our own. Yet the LORD laid on him the sins of us all." Type that on a piece of paper and show it to your non-Christian friends. Ask them who it's about and where it comes from. One person who tried this found that everyone said, "It is obviously Jesus of Nazareth, that's who it is. And it is from the New Testament."[1] But actually it comes from the book of Isaiah (53:6) in the Hebrew Bible and was written about seven centuries before the life and death of Christ. In fact, read all of Isaiah 53 and try to comprehend that the words "he was pierced for our rebellion, crushed for our sins" (53:5) were written centuries before the Romans had even invented the practice of nailing a criminal's hands and feet to a cross. Jesus' life fulfills dozens of such Old Testament predictions in ways that Jesus and his followers could not have manipulated nor invented. These point overwhelmingly to the divine authorship of the Bible—as well as the divine identity of Jesus, the Messiah.

2. Give each person a chance to talk about the arrow that draws their attention the most. Share with the group:

   • What do you find compelling about that argument?

   • Do you know anyone who would be helped by hearing this evidence—or perhaps having a fuller explanation of this line of thinking?

   • Would it be helpful for you to learn more about these arrows from *Choosing Your Faith* or another source?

Different arrows will appeal to different group members. That's okay. And it's okay to ask questions about the arrows that you don't understand or don't find helpful. After all, these are very brief summaries that leave out a lot of the information and evidence behind them.

Next, here are four arrows pointing powerfully to the truth that Jesus was the Son of God:

Arrow 13: Jesus' sinless life backed up his claim to be the Son of God. A merely human leader doesn't need to be perfect in order to be followed, but someone who claims to be the Son of God would certainly need to be. The New Testament accounts portray a man with a full-blooded personality but no character flaws, ethical inconsistencies, or even human errors. As a result, Jesus' enemies and desperate accusers couldn't indict him on any moral or criminal grounds other than what they considered to be blasphemy—based on his claims to be God's Son. This is also the charge leveled against him in Jewish references from the first few centuries AD. But if his claim to be God's Son was true, then he was innocent. No other major religious leader ever claimed to be sinless, and only one consistently lived like it—Jesus.

Arrow 14: Jesus' resurrection powerfully established his credentials as the Son of God. He was executed and buried, but three days later his tomb was empty. Even his enemies admitted that the corpse had disappeared. They claimed his disciples stole the body while the soldiers guarding the tomb slept. But why would those terrified men in danger of being similarly arrested and executed stick their necks out for what they would have known was a hoax? Further, how did those soldiers know the disciples had stolen the body if they were sleeping at the time? And if they weren't sleeping, why didn't they stop the theft? The story just doesn't add up! In addition, numerous men and women reported seeing, talking to, and even eating with the risen Jesus—over a period of several weeks. None of them profited by telling the story, and many went to horrible deaths because they insisted their entire lives that they had met the risen Jesus. Why would they do that, other than for the obvious answer: It was the truth!

Arrow 16: The changed lives of early skeptics affirmed the truth of Jesus' resurrection and the teachings of the church. Not only did Jesus' friends believe the extraordinary story of his return from death, but even some who at first aggressively opposed the story later changed their minds, including masses of religious opponents in Jerusalem in Acts 2. And there was Saul, for example, who was enthusiastically hunting down and arresting those who were calling Jesus the Messiah. But then Saul had an encounter with Jesus, who was very much alive, and this completely turned him around. He abandoned his promising career, began to use the name Paul, and dedicated the rest of his life, at great personal sacrifice and eventual martyrdom, to spreading the message of Christ. Paul's changed life alone gives powerful evidence to the truth of Jesus' resurrection and to the message of the gospel.

Arrow 17: The willingness of the disciples to die for claims they knew to be true affirms the trustworthiness of their claims. Most of Jesus' original twelve disciples were brutally executed for refusing to renounce their claim of having personally seen his miracles before he died and having seen him alive after his death. Paul too was eventually executed for his claim of firsthand experience with the living Christ. Either they were telling the truth, or they were flatly lying and they knew it. *But nobody dies for what they know to be a lie!* Yes, there are terrorists today who die for the lie that God will reward them for killing innocent people. But here's the difference: They think it's true but don't have any way of knowing for sure—until it's too late, at the judgment. The disciples, on the other hand, did know for sure about the truth of their claims to have spent time with the risen Christ. And their willingness to give up everything—including life itself—to uphold their testimony about him speaks *volumes* about the truthfulness of their claims.

3. Again, give each person a chance to talk about the one or two arrows that they think will be most helpful in talking to friends about their faith. Share with the group:

- What do you find compelling about that argument?

- Do you know anyone who would be helped by this line of thinking?

- Would it be helpful for you to learn more about these arrows from *Choosing Your Faith* or another source?

Have someone watch the clock so that each person has a chance to talk, and so that you save twenty minutes at the end of your meeting for the second half of the video and for prayer. The leader of the whole group or class should keep track of the time and call everyone back to view the second part of the video.

Play DVD segment 2 of Session 7: Elements of a Confident Faith, Part 2—More Arrows of Truth

Write your notes from the DVD here:

Prayer

Go back to your prayer circle to pray for one another.

I passed on to you what was most important and what had also been passed on to me. Christ died for our sins, just as the Scriptures said. He was buried, and he was raised from the dead on the third day, just as the Scriptures said. He was seen by Peter and then by the Twelve. After that, he was seen by more than 500 of his followers at one time, most of whom are still alive, though some have died. Then he was seen by James and later by all the apostles. Last of all, as though I had been born at the wrong time, I also saw him. (1 Corinthians 15:3–8)

Share what you got out of the video of Mark and the picture he drew, as well as the information in these last two sessions, as we've looked at these arrows of evidence for the Christian faith. Was it helpful to you? Then tell the circle how they can pray for you. Do you feel able to begin explaining some of this kind of information with your non-Christian friends? Do you want to thank God for strengthening your faith? Do you need encouragement to follow through to learn more? Do you need courage to share some of this evidence with someone you know?

Pray for each person in your circle.

Coming up in session 8: People often say they doubt the Christian message for intellectual reasons, but often their barriers to faith are emotional and spiritual. What are some of those barriers, and how can you help your friends get past them?

Reminder: Reading chapters 10 and 11 of *Choosing Your Faith* before we meet again will help you better understand the ideas we've covered in this session.

For Further Reading on the Evidence for the Christian Faith

Choosing Your Faith by Mark Mittelberg (Tyndale, 2008)

The Case for Christ by Lee Strobel (Zondervan, 1998)

The Case for Faith by Lee Strobel (Zondervan, 2000)

The Case for a Creator by Lee Strobel (Zondervan, 2004)

The Case for the Real Jesus by Lee Strobel (Zondervan, 2007)

The Case for the Resurrection of Jesus by Gary R. Habermas and Michael R. Licona (Kregel, 2004)

More Than a Carpenter, rev. ed., by Josh and Sean McDowell (Tyndale, 2009)

Know Why You Believe, rev. ed., by Paul Little (InterVarsity, 2008)

Jesus Among Other Gods by Ravi Zacharias (W Publishing, 2000)

The Creator and the Cosmos by Hugh Ross (NavPress, 1993)

The Historical Jesus: Ancient Evidence for the Life of Christ by Gary Habermas (College Press, 1996)

The New Testament Documents: Are They Reliable? by F. F. Bruce (Eerdmans, 1981)

When Skeptics Ask by Norman Geisler and Ronald Brooks (Baker, 2008)

Session 8

HELPING FRIENDS OVERCOME
THEIR BARRIERS TO FAITH

It would be wonderful if helping our friends figure out what to believe were as easy as simply laying out the facts and information in front of them. But it isn't usually so. Maybe people *should* decide what to believe based on an objective study of the evidence, but almost nobody actually *does*. Most people who resist trusting in Christ have a mixture of intellectual, emotional, and spiritual barriers between them and God. So rather than trying to argue our friends into a faith commitment, we need to lovingly help them identify and work through their emotional and spiritual barriers as well. In this session we'll look at ten potential barriers and consider how we can help our friends overcome them.

Before the DVD

1. Think of a non-Christian you know. If that person were to give one reason for not following Christ, what might it be?

For more information on the material covered in this session, please read chapters 12 and 13 of *Choosing Your Faith*.

Play DVD segment Session 8: Helping Friends Overcome Their Barriers to Faith

Write your notes from the DVD here:

After the DVD

In previous sessions we've talked about *intellectual* barriers people sometimes face when they consider the claims of Christ: their need for information, evidence, and answers to their doubts. In this session's DVD, Mark addressed ten common *emotional* and *spiritual* barriers people sometimes face. These ten barriers are:

- **Lack of openness.** Their presuppositions and prejudices keep them from being open to new information that radically challenges their view of the world.

- **Lifestyle issues.** They don't want to give up habits such as immoral sexual activities, unethical business practices, or addictions that they know are inconsistent with Christian teachings.

- **Personal hurts.** They've been hurt by Christians or church leaders, or they've experienced suffering that makes them question or even reject the existence of a good God.

- **Desire for control.** They deeply want to be in control of their own lives and hate the thought of yielding any of their freedom to a higher power, even if he is the God of the universe.

- **Anger.** They get angry at the suggestion that their religion is wrong, their holy books and spiritual leaders are misguided, or that their family and the culture they grew up in have been on the wrong track.

- **Discomfort with change.** They're uncomfortable with change in general.

- **Fear.** They're afraid, perhaps hearing an inner voice that says, "You've got too much to do before letting go of your freedom and putting on a religious straitjacket." Or a whisper from Satan telling them, "You're unworthy and beyond the reach of grace."

- **Disinterest in faith and truth.** They simply don't care about issues of truth and faith. "Whatever" is their motto.

- **Oversimplicity.** The idea of just humbling themselves to receive God's grace—without needing to work or pay for it—seems too simple to be true. Grace can't be *that* amazing, can it?

- **Lack of spiritual experience.** They haven't had a personal spiritual experience of feeling God's presence or sensing Christ's concern and love for them.

2. What spiritual barriers did you have to overcome in your own journey to Christ? (If you've been a Christian since childhood, perhaps you've encountered some barriers in staying true to your faith as you've grown up.)

3. Think of three non-Christians you know. Take a moment on your own to write down their names and one or more of the barriers listed above (or perhaps others that weren't listed) that you think might be the biggest obstacles for each of them.

Name:

Barrier(s):

Name:

Barrier(s):

Name:

Barrier(s):

4. Now, without necessarily saying their names, share with your group the barriers you listed for each person.

Having identified the barriers, let's think about ways we can try to help our friends overcome them. Below are some examples of things we can do for each barrier.

- **Lack of openness.** We can build a genuine friendship with them to the point where we have built enough trust to gently mention that this seems to be an issue for them. Sometimes the loving nudges of someone who really cares can help a person open up. We should also pray for them about this.

- **Lifestyle issues.** Again, we can spend time building a relationship of trust, expose them to teaching opportunities and materials that will challenge their lifestyle, and, as God leads, humbly and gently confront the issues that are standing between them and him. Again, we can also pray.

- **Personal hurts.** We need to do lots of listening and praying while demonstrating genuine care. Through our loving behavior and approach, we can show our friends what Jesus is really like while reminding them that he cares about them and what they've been through. We can also introduce our friends to other Christians who, like us, don't fit their negative stereotypes from past experience. If suffering has made them doubt whether there can be a good God, we can investigate and share with them Christian answers to the problem of suffering, but we need to remember that intellectual answers don't touch the ache of a wounded heart. Often what's needed most is just a loving and caring friend.

- **Desire for control.** This is another issue that requires a lot of prayer and patience before we address it. Sometimes circumstances (such as strife in their marriage or workplace relationships) give us an opening to draw our friend's attention to their controlling nature—along with the negative impact it's having on their relationships with others, and with God. But it's important to have first earned the right to be honest (through consistent demonstrations of care and respect), or we're likely to provoke defensiveness.

- **Anger.** Again, we'll need patience and prayer and a foundation of friendship before trying to put the mirror up to let them see their problem. But they need to see it, along with the cost they're paying relationally and especially spiritually.

- **Discomfort with change.** We can help our friend put words to this problem. Often just talking about it together—and explaining to them how your own willingness to change worked out for the best—can help break down this barrier.

- **Fear.** Again, we can talk about this and help our friends open up about their concerns and fears—while reassuring them with our words and stories of overcoming spiritual fears ourselves. We can also pray that as they get closer to trusting in God, his perfect love will expel all of their fears (1 John 4:18).

- **Disinterest in faith and truth.** We can pray and wait for circumstances that will help our friend see that their attitude of "whatever" isn't helping whatsoever! We can also remind them of the eternal importance of spiritual matters, seeking to shake them out of their complacency.

- **Oversimplicity.** We can explain that there is a natural tendency to think we must learn more, give more, earn more, pay more—because there is, as it's often stated, no free lunch! So, many people reason, there's got to be more to getting right with God than just trusting in Jesus. Well, there actually was more to it, but God handled the hard parts by sending Jesus to pay the price for our sin in our place on the cross. That leaves the simpler part to us: trusting in him for his forgiveness and leadership. That's why John 1:12 promises, "But to all who believed him and accepted him, he gave the right to become children of God."

- **Lack of spiritual experience.** We can invite our friends to go places with us that will expose them to good teaching, genuine worship, and interaction with sincere followers of Christ. This might be church services, special classes or seminars, Christian movies or concerts, or our small group. It's amazing what getting in the right environment can do to further a person's spiritual progress.

(Note: If your friends' barriers are intellectual, such as doubt whether God exists, here are some ideas: You can talk with your friends about information you've found helpful and invite them to classes or small-group opportunities where they'll learn more. You can also give them a book, such as *Choosing Your Faith* (which was written especially for non-Christians) or one of the other books listed at the end of session 7. You can look in these books for ways of addressing your friends' honest questions. You can reason with them, not trying to win a debate but truly listening to them and respectfully replying. You can invite them to read passages of the Bible with you and have an open and honest discussion.)

5. Look back at the barriers you listed in question 3. What are two or three ideas for things you can do to help your friends overcome their barriers?

6. What obstacles do you face in building the kinds of friendships in which barriers like hurt, fear, anger, and the desire for control can be addressed? What practical things can you do, even this week, to deepen the relationship and begin to address these obstacles?

7. Sometimes it's easier to build friendships with non-Christians if you partner with other Christians than if you go it alone. With a team, you can find multiple areas of common interest, backgrounds, etc. Also, you don't have to have all the gifts or experience to address every barrier, and you can stay more motivated to pray when nothing seems to be changing in your friend's life.

   How can those in your group help each other in deepening relationships and perhaps doing things together with the non-Christians you know? (*Examples: You could commit to keep praying for each other and for the unbelievers in your lives. You could plan a dinner or outing with others from your group and a few of your non-Christian friends.*)

8. What is one valuable thing you've gained from this group over the past eight sessions?

9. Celebrate the completion of this training process by doing something fun together. What might that be?

_____

Reminder: Reading the last part of *Choosing Your Faith,* chapters 12 and 13, will help you better understand the ideas we've covered in this session.

Prayer

_____

If you're in a discussion group larger than eight people, subdivide into circles of four or five people for prayer.

_____

Pray for the non-Christians in your lives. Pray specifically about the barriers that stand between them and Christ, and pray for ways to strengthen your relationships with them. Ask God to help you overcome things like busyness and fear that can keep us from spending time with non-Christians. Ask for the boldness and clarity you'll need to help these people find a path to faith that will lead them to Christ and his amazing gifts of forgiveness, leadership, and life that never ends.

LEADER'S GUIDE

Few experiences in the Christian life are more thrilling than helping someone who has been wandering down a dead-end lane change direction and start walking toward Christ. And if you're leading a group through this training series, you're helping each person in your group prepare for that experience. This series is discussion driven, not teacher driven, so you don't have to be an expert in the topics we'll discuss or in leading people to Christ. All you need is the willingness to prepare each week, guide the discussion, and rely on the Holy Spirit to work in your heart and the hearts of group members.

Large and Small Groups

This series can be used effectively in groups of any size.

If your group includes two to twelve people, you can stay together as one group for your whole discussion. We suggest that you arrange your chairs in a U shape around the television so that everyone can see the screen while you watch the DVD portions and so that everyone can see each other's face as you discuss your thoughts before and after the DVD. You will be the facilitator for the discussion. See below for guidelines on facilitating a discussion.

If your group includes thirteen to three hundred people, you can arrange chairs in rows for the opening icebreaker questions and for viewing the DVD. After you view the DVD, ask participants to move chairs and gather in circles of four or five people for discussion. Smaller circles allow everyone plenty of time to talk. Also, people who are shy about talking in large groups are often more comfortable talking in small ones. And people who tend to dominate discussions in large groups are more easily balanced out by others in small circles.

Each of these smaller circles will need a facilitator. Facilitators don't need to be experts either in the content matter or in leading groups, because they will fairly quickly learn how to guide a circle with only three or four other people. Circles can often choose the most natural facilitator among them after getting to know each other for only a brief time. In your first meeting, after circles have formed, ask everyone to look at the guidelines for facilitators below. Or you can read these guidelines aloud. Circles will often unanimously choose someone among them to do the job once they know what it involves.

It's a good idea to stick with the same circle for the whole series, so that members get to know each other. Encourage people to attend consistently so that circles remain intact.

Facilitating the Discussion

The facilitator's job isn't to have all the answers. He or she simply needs to …

- keep the circle on track when it's tempted to go off on a tangent;

- keep the discussion moving so that it doesn't get stuck on one question;

- make sure that everyone gets a chance to talk and that no one dominates (it is not necessary that every person respond aloud to every question, but every person should have the chance to do so);

- make sure that the discussion remains respectful.

The discussion should be a conversation among the group members, not a one-on-one with the facilitator. The facilitator can encourage this with statements like, "Allison said X. What do others of you think?" A facilitator should wait for others' responses before jumping in with his or her own response to a question. Facilitators should also be comfortable with silence; it usually means people are thinking.

Many questions invite the group to brainstorm ideas. There is space in the workbook to write down these ideas. The facilitator should encourage group members to do so. But if people are so focused on writing that they can't participate in the discussion, you may want to rotate the task of recording ideas.

Some people think best by saying ideas aloud. Others think best by forming ideas inside their heads, or writing them down, and then sharing them. It's a good idea to allow some silence for those who think best by writing or reflecting silently. Or let them listen to the discussion, and then, after a while, invite their thoughts. You may even find that if you give them some airtime at the beginning of your next meeting, they will have valuable ideas about last week's discussion.

In some cases, as with the quizzes in sessions 2 through 5, the workbook will instruct everyone to write answers on their own. If there is no instruction to write answers, then the question is for group discussion. Participants can make notes if they like, but the idea is to keep the discussion moving.

Facilitating the Prayer Time

Each session ends with prayer in smaller circles. Even if you have twelve people in your group and are discussing the questions as one body, it's a good idea to move to smaller circles for prayer so that everyone can participate. (Groups that feel strongly about hearing all the prayer requests can have circles write them down and share them afterward.)

Some group members may never have prayed aloud in front of others. Make sure everyone knows it is okay to pray silently or to pray just one sentence aloud.

Encourage group members to be open in asking for prayer. Also, they don't need to name their non-Christian friends if they prefer not to. Emphasize this ground rule that applies to the entire discussion:

> *Confidentiality: Whatever is said in the group stays in the group. Nothing is to be repeated to those who weren't there.*

Most sessions include a passage of Scripture that you can turn into a prayer if you need help with words. In session 1, for example, a prayer based on Philippians 1:9–10 might sound like this if a person was having conflicts with one of his coworkers:

> *I pray that Steve's love for the guy in the office next to his will overflow more and more. Please keep him growing in knowledge and understanding of you, Father, and of other people. Help him know what really matters and stay focused on that, especially in his dealings with his coworker.*

Materials Needed

Each group member will need a copy of this workbook. You may want to buy all the workbooks and distribute them, asking for a donation to cover the cost or funding the workbooks out of your church's evangelism, missions, or education budget.

Each group member would benefit from reading the book *Choosing Your Faith*. Every workbook session points out the chapter of *Choosing Your Faith* that contains more information on the material covered in that session. As a leader, you will find it extremely valuable to read the book. It's not essential that group members read the book, but they will get a lot out of it, and you should encourage them to read it. Also, *Choosing Your Faith* is written with non-Christian readers in mind, so it's an ideal book for group members to give to family and friends. This workbook discusses nonthreatening ways of giving the book to a non-Christian. You might want to buy a supply of books and have them available for group members to read or give away.

Each group member will also need a pen or pencil to make notes and respond to quizzes. You might want to bring a handful to your first meeting in case people need them.

Leader Preparation

As leader, you should view the DVD segment and read the workbook material (including material in this leader's guide) for each session before the group meets. Think about how you would answer the questions. In this way you'll be prepared for what's coming, and you won't be distracted by needing to consult the leader's guide as often during the meeting.

Ideally, facilitators of small circles should also review the workbook and leader's guide before each meeting. If that's unrealistic, you can let them consult the leader's guide as they go along, or in some cases you can give instructions from the front of the room.

Before each meeting, make sure the chairs are set up for viewing the DVD. Also, double-check the television and DVD player to be certain they are working (things happen!), and cue up the DVD to the segment you're going to view so that the group doesn't have to wait while you navigate through the menu.

Session 1

Open the meeting with a prayer.

The main takeaways from this session are:

- Faith is both belief and action that are based on something we consider to be trustworthy, even though we don't have absolute proof.

- Everyone lives by faith, including people who claim they don't.

Question 1. The first question in every session is an icebreaker. Its main purpose is to help people relax, feel welcome, and transition from their busy lives to the topic they're going to discuss. A second purpose is to help people get to know each other. If your group comprises two to twelve people, you can let everyone share their answers with the whole group. If your group is larger or if you are pressed for time, ask members to share their answers with a couple of people sitting near them. Ask them to keep their answers brief. A group of twelve people should spend no more than ten minutes on this question, and you should need only about two minutes if people are just sharing with a couple of people sitting near them.

View the DVD segment. At the end of the DVD segment, a question will be on the screen. That is the first question you'll discuss when you turn off the DVD. It is also in the workbook, so participants don't need to worry about forgetting it if they have to move their chairs.

Question 2. Ask people to avoid telling long stories (until after the meeting time!), but to answer this question in a few sentences. You might want to model an appropriate response for the whole group. Plan ahead of time an answer that is light, perhaps funny, and no more than three sentences.

Definition of faith. Draw attention to the definition of faith: *Faith is belief and action that are based on something we consider to be trustworthy, even though we don't have absolute proof.* That something might be an object, like your car; an idea, like democracy; or a person, like somebody you love or look up to, or the God who made you.

Question 4. Presumably you have enough faith in the chair you're sitting in to sit in it. When you sat down, you trusted it not to collapse. You probably trust electricity to work in certain ways, and although you may not know anything about how it works, you demonstrate your faith each time you plug something in or flip a switch.

Ask someone in the group to read aloud the text that begins "Everybody has faith …" while others read along silently.

Questions 5–6. Allow two or three minutes for participants to write answers. Then invite them to share—not every word of what they wrote, but what they learned, what they noticed about others, how the people they listed are similar or different.

Question 7. Most people are fuzzy about what they believe and unaware of why they believe it. This series will help you become more aware of what you believe and why it makes sense—and more able to help the people around you to think through these things and get on the path toward faith in Christ.

Session 2

Open with prayer.

The main takeaways from this session are:

- Relativism is a viewpoint that says truth or reality is merely a subjective by-product of the mind. It's something you invent, not something you discover.

- If relativism is reasonable, then why not invent/choose to believe things merely because they work for you, serve your needs, and fit with other things you believe? Many people in our culture do just that—regardless of hard facts.

- Relativism assumes there are no moral absolutes that are right for everyone. But relativists tend to feel strongly about one moral absolute: You should not judge other people's beliefs or try to impose your beliefs on them.

- Relativism doesn't make logical sense. Some things are real and true whether we like or believe in them or not. We can invent our own fantasy worlds, but we can't create reality.

- It's important to love truth and seek it wholeheartedly.

Ask several people to take turns reading aloud the introductory text beginning on the first page of this session—this is pivotal information that sets up what you'll be discussing for the rest of the course. The idea that different people think in different ways may seem foreign to some group members, but as you hear the various people on the DVD over the next several weeks, you'll see how differently they approached life before they came to Christ.

Question 2. Make sure everyone has something to write with. Tell people not to spend a lot of time overthinking and evaluating these statements, but to write down their immediate reaction. The point here is to get a general sense of their natural tendencies. Ask them not to discuss their answers at this point. When most people are finished, turn on the DVD.

After the DVD. Read aloud the paragraph under the heading "After the DVD." Then, if your group is larger than twelve people, ask participants to move into their smaller circles. They can spend the first few minutes in their circles talking about what they learned about themselves from the quiz. If they didn't like it, they can say so! Ask them to explain why.

Question 3. This word *judgmental* is enormously negative in our culture. Our culture leans toward relativism, and "judgmentalism" is a very bad quality from a relativistic point of view. (However, relativists can feel very strongly that they're right about what is and isn't judgmental. And they often don't see that they're trying to impose a right and wrong that they consider to be true for everyone—and can be quite judgmental about it!)

Jesus warns us against judging others in the sense of claiming the right to be their final judge, with the right to condemn them (Matthew 7:1–2). In these verses he speaks against arrogance, presumption, and harshness. However, in many other places he urges us to have good judgment in the sense of wise discernment. We need to be able to judge, for example, whether a teacher is teaching truth or falsehood (Matthew 7:15–20).

Question 4. Matters of opinion are one thing—pistachio ice cream may taste good to you but not to me, or you may think that Napoleon was a great leader rather than a tyrant. But neither differing opinions nor relativistic beliefs change the reality of the actual facts— either Napoleon was defeated at Waterloo or he wasn't. Either George Washington chopped down a cherry tree and refused to tell a lie, or he didn't. (In fact, he didn't. That's a fable that historians have disproved.) Christianity is based on historical events that either did or didn't happen, and on ideas about the universe that are true for everybody or nobody (see under question 5). If these events didn't happen, then Christianity is a fable that nobody should believe. The apostle Paul makes this point in 1 Corinthians 15:17–19.

Question 5. God can't exist on one side of a room and not exist on the other side just because nobody on that other side believes in him. He either exists or not—in both places. Jesus either rose from the dead or he didn't—this is a question about a historical event that either happened or didn't happened. We can't say, for example, "World War II happened for you but not for me." Reports of historical events can vary in accuracy, but the event itself happened in a particular way, and the job of historians is to find out what really occurred as best they can. Likewise, either humans are sinful and need a Savior (a Christian belief), or else that understanding is incorrect. These are all Christian beliefs that are either true for everybody or not true at all.

Ask someone to read aloud the text following question 5 that begins "We need to be clear …"

Question 6. For example, they have to give up the illusion that they control their reality. They may have to give up some beliefs that have justified their putting their own desires and interests first. The central issue is control.

Question 7. We no longer live in a society where most people come from the same background and share the same religious and cultural beliefs. We live in a global and mobile society where people of vastly different backgrounds interact all the time. Relativism may help people maintain harmonious relationships with those who have drastically different views on what is real, what is important in life, and what is right and wrong—but that "help" comes at the great cost of blurring understandings of truth itself. And certainly we can, and should, be tolerant toward others—even if we're convinced their ideas are wrong. But we must be careful to never confuse tolerance with truth.

Question 9. Relativists often deflect attempts to talk about evidence. They believe evidence isn't objectively real and so can be dismissed if they don't want to entertain it. Also, they believe it is bad manners or even immoral to try to persuade someone to abandon their beliefs in favor of other ones. And Christianity is the main belief system that angers some relativists, because they see Christians as often abusing power.

Question 10. It's important to build relationships with people and to go into a conversation like this focused on winning the person, not the argument. That is, we're trying to win them to a deeper relationship of care and respect, as well as gently urging them to consider our point of view. If we have our attitude straight, then we can casually say, "I heard this interesting thing in a class I'm taking. Can I tell you about it and see what you think?"

Question 11. You might pray for God to open their minds to perceive what is real and to show them the logical contradictions in their ideas. You could pray based on 2 Corinthians 4:4. You could ask God to put them in situations that will show them that they need to choose what to believe in and not keep avoiding the choice.

Session 3

The main takeaways from this session are:

- The Traditional approach adopts beliefs based on the religious practices (or lack thereof) we learned from our families.

- The Authoritarian path is similar in that it is usually passively received. The difference between the two is that the Traditional approach is more about a habit that gets passed down from one generation to the next, whereas the Authoritarian approach is based on submission to a religious leader, teacher, or organization and the ideas this authority holds up as true.

- Both traditions and authorities have their place in the Christian life, but we need to test them with logic and evidence to make sure they are reliable.

Question 2. Make sure everyone has something to write with. Tell people not to spend a lot of time overthinking these quiz statements, but to write down their immediate reaction.

After the DVD. Invite group members to share their answers to the quiz. (If you have a large group, you could have people raise their hands and volunteer to share if they want to. It's not necessary for everyone to share their results.)

You may have a lot of traditionalists in your group and maybe some who are drawn to the Authoritarian faith path. Make sure everyone understands that it's not bad to value Christian tradition and Christian authorities. But we need to test even those traditions and authorities to be sure they are reliable. For instance, it's possible to have a mostly accurate Christian tradition along with some dos and don'ts that come from our subculture rather than the Scriptures.

It's not necessary to belabor the group's answers to the quiz. After a few minutes, read aloud the paragraph under the heading "After the DVD." Then, if your group is larger than twelve people, ask participants to move into their smaller circles to start question 3.

Question 3. Tradition gives us many good things, such as roots, stability, and a sense of belonging. Many Christian doctrines come from a tradition of wise people studying the Scriptures and then articulating and passing down biblical doctrines, such as the nature of Christ—that he is fully God, equal to the Father, as well as fully human. We don't have to reinvent every wheel of theology and practical Christian living.

Question 4. Jesus notes two problems: (1) We can have hearts far from God and still go through the motions of a tradition—but God is interested in our hearts. (2) We can do what our misguided tradition tells us instead of what God tells us. We need to entertain the possibility that our parents could have been (even partly) wrong in the beliefs and practices they taught us.

Question 5. We need to test our traditions by logic and evidence (including, but not limited to, evidence from the Bible). We need to make sure they don't contradict or hinder things God has told us to do. And we need to make sure that our traditions aid us, not distract or divert us, in bringing our hearts near to God.

Question 6. While a person on the Traditional faith path may just inherit customs or ideas passed on from generation to generation, the Authoritarian approach is based on submission to a religious authority, whether that be a person, an organization, or a book—or, most often, a combination of these.

Ask someone to read aloud the text following question 7 that begins "As we heard …" Group members can read the material in the shaded box following that paragraph on their own later.

Questions 9–10. Because some people derive a great deal of their identity from the tradition or authority they come from or have adopted, challenging it threatens to dismantle their identity. It can be very uncomfortable, even threatening, to have elements of our core identity questioned. It's important that we don't attack someone's tradition, because that comes across as attacking their identity, who they are. Instead, we need to come alongside them as real friends, demonstrate genuine care, give up a desire to win an argument, and engage them in constructive spiritual conversation. Perhaps we can tell the story of how we have investigated a tradition we grew up with and how that was uncomfortable but ultimately helpful. We can talk about how we've found it valuable to test our own beliefs—resulting in either the affirmation of what we'd been taught or giving us the impetus to explore further and perhaps make some needed changes. We can also ask them gentle but probing questions about their traditions.

Session 4

The main takeaways from this session are:

- People who take the Intuitive faith path tend not to trust in their intellect or what their eyes and ears tell them. They trust an inner sense that they believe points them toward right ideas and actions.

- Those on the Mystical path believe they gain spiritual understanding through direct communication from God or his messengers.

- People can have valid intuitions and mystical experiences, but not everything we feel is real, and not everything real is good. Therefore, it's essential to test these experiences to see if they're truly from God and to pay healthy attention to what our intellect and senses are saying.

Question 1. This is an icebreaker intended to make group members aware of differences in personality in a general way. To some degree, intuition or lack of it is a personality trait. The Intuitive faith path is different from having intuitive abilities, and as we critique that faith path, it will be important for group members to know that we are not criticizing their personality. Question 1 doesn't get at this issue directly, but it does open the subject of personality differences. Also, it's not necessary for anyone to try to summarize his or her entire personality in two or three words!

Question 3. It's possible that humans have varying levels of built-in intuitive instinct that works with our other senses—and perhaps sometimes independently—to give us quick and clear impressions of dangers, opportunities, or direction. Intuition can alert us to these things in a general way, but it usually doesn't tell us what to do.

Question 4. Be prepared for some pushback. The idea of trusting the heart rather than the senses is very popular. Assure people that we're not saying they should ignore their hearts, only that they should pay attention to their minds and senses and the other sources of information they bring as well (including the message of the Bible). You might need to remind them that the Bible warns that our natural heart is "deceitful above all things" (Jeremiah 17:9 NIV).

Ask someone to read aloud the text following question 4 that begins "Beyond simple intuitive awareness …"

After you discuss question 6, ask someone to read aloud the text following that question that begins "Intuition can be the flashing yellow light …" Note that in this text the symbol ≠ should be read to mean "does not necessarily equal." We're not using it to say "never equals." We're definitely not saying that feelings never point to something real, or that real mystical experiences are never good!

Question 5. Simply put, the promises often don't deliver. Romances can go sour when we discover that the person has huge debts, or a gambling addiction, or a violent temper. The investment opportunity that we didn't check out because we had a good feeling about the broker can cost us thousands (con men know how to make people feel comfortable). Intuition is a great tool in partnership with fact-checking, but on its own it can lead to costly mistakes.

Question 7. A classic example would be feeling that someone you've just met is the love of your life—that feeling isn't always reliable. Likewise, an emotional high from an evening with great music and a talented speaker isn't necessarily a real experience of God.

Question 8. Deuteronomy 18:9–11 forbids consulting the dead, and many believe consulting the dead is impossible. But 1 Samuel 28 seems to suggest that the witch of Endor did make contact with the dead prophet Samuel, not a demon or fraud. But it's clear from the story that however real this paranormal event was, it wasn't good or of God.

Questions 10–11. These can be profound, private experiences that not everyone will want to share. So be sensitive to the participants' desire for privacy. On the other hand, if someone goes on and on with a story, you'll need to discern when to gently cut in and apologize for the fact that the discussion needs to move on to the final prayer soon.

It would be good to point out that these stories offer an opportunity for group members to team up with each other in their relationships with non-Christian friends. If someone in the group has a friend who is on a Mystical path, and someone else in the group has had mystical or intuitive experiences (whether positive or negative), you can ask if the latter person would be willing to share their experience with the first person's friend. Maybe the two group members and the mystical friend could share a meal together or meet for dessert in one of their homes.

Between questions 11 and 12 have someone read the section after question 11, starting with "Another way of starting a conversation …"

Session 5

The main takeaways from this session are:

- The Evidential faith path provides the criteria for testing the ideas gained through all five of the other paths.

- The two inescapable elements of this faith path are logic and sensory experience, or evidence.

- We need to intentionally use these God-given tools throughout our lives, and we need to help our friends understand why they are vitally important.

- One vital principle of logic is the law of non-contradiction, which asserts that two conflicting statements can't both be true.

After you discuss question 4, ask someone to read aloud the text following that question with the heading "The Law of Non-Contradiction."

Question 4. The key reasons are:

- We can't think, evaluate ideas, or make decisions without logic.

- Even those who claim we can't trust logic use logic to try to make their point.

- People in the East use logic just as people in the West do.

- Deuteronomy 13 tells us to use logic to test a prophet.

- Galatians 1:8–9 tells us to use logic to test someone's version of the gospel.

- Even those who say you can't trust sensory experience (sight, sound, etc.) use their senses to try to prove their point.

- We rely on evidence to determine what's true in the realms of science, history, and courts of law, so why not in the spiritual realm too?

- Jesus often told people to look at the evidence of his life in order to verify his claims.

Give people plenty of time to voice their resistance to using logic and sensory experience to verify their intuitions, mystical experiences, etc. It's very important not to shut people down, as that won't change the way they live when they leave the group. You may need to emphasize that we're not arguing that evidence should replace intuition, authority, etc. We're arguing that wise people learn to use it alongside those other ways of knowing. And even people who feel they're not good at logic can learn to use it and can rely on the help of those who are better at it, just as people who aren't good at intuition can develop it and pay attention to others who are better at it.

Question 5. This is an exercise in logic. Many people say things like "All the major religions are true ways to God." To respond to such statements effectively, we need to know enough about the different religions to be aware of some of the key beliefs that contradict one another. You might ask your friend who says this, "Christianity says Jesus is the Son of God, as he claims to be in the New Testament. Islam says he isn't the Son of God and never claimed to be. Is there a way both of these beliefs can be true?" You may find yourself in a discussion of whether the law of non-contradiction is valid. You can give the example of the gas tank.

The goal here is to learn to see and talk about the contradictions in one's own beliefs and other people's beliefs—and to do so not in the spirit of scoring points for winning an argument, but in the spirit of caring about another person. Our primary aim should not be to prove people wrong but to win hearts to God. Can you see the contradictions between these three religions? Can you see why Jesus can't *be* the Jewish Messiah and *not be* the Jewish Messiah?

Question 6. It's important that we respect each other and get along peacefully. But respect and peace don't require agreement. You can explain that the identity of Jesus lies at the heart of Christian faith. If Jesus is who he claims to be in the New Testament, then our lives in this world and the next depend on our believing his claims and doing what he asks of us (see, for example, what he says about this in John 8:24). If he isn't who he claimed, then the New Testament is a fraud, and it would be tragic to base one's life on what it teaches. Jesus teaches us to do things that anybody would consider wise (like controlling our tempers) but also things that go against our best interest unless the New Testament is reliable (Luke 9:23–26 is an example).

Incidentally, the same is true of Islam and every other religion. If Islam is right about Muhammad and all he taught, then it's critically important for all of us to do what the Quran says, not what the Bible says in areas where they disagree, and not whatever you feel like doing. But if Islam is wrong, then millions of people are making a tragic mistake in the way they live their lives.

Ask several people to take turns reading aloud the text following question 6 that begins "On the other hand …" Each person can read a paragraph. Read also the paragraphs under the heading "The Arbitrary Limiting of Evidence." Before you go on to question 7, ask whether anybody has questions about this material. Some may find it complicated, so see if the group can help everyone understand what is being said (you can also consult the last section of chapter 7 of *Choosing Your Faith* for more information).

Question 8. This is difficult, because people resist facing that they even have assumptions. But the main thing to do is to help your friend see that the belief that the scientific method is the only method for discovering truth is an arbitrary and unprovable assumption. There may be pragmatic reasons for looking only for natural causes in many kinds of scientific research, but that's not the same as proving that supernatural beings/causes don't and can't exist. Science never disproves God—in fact, as we'll see in the next session, science often points powerfully toward God's existence—but some scientists try to rule God out by definition (which is very unscientific!).

Session 6

The main takeaways from this session are:

- God does speak through mystical experiences, intuition, tradition, and authorities. But it's essential that we use logic and evidence to test these sources of beliefs, so that we'll know which ones are trustworthy and which aren't.

- There is plenty of information and evidence to support the belief that a wise and powerful Creator God exists. It's important to help our non-Christian

friends come to see why evidence like this is valuable—and points toward
the Christian understanding of God.

The first half of this session is a review of the idea of using evidence to test information from
the other five paths. The second half begins to look at some of the evidence. Hopefully, by now
everyone in your group will understand why being aware of this evidence is valuable. Some
may still feel that they know what they believe and that they don't need more reasons than
they already have. For them, two points: (1) There are more and more voices in our culture
bent on challenging our beliefs; knowing this information will strengthen the foundations of
their faith and make them more confident, even against strong opposition. (2) They probably
know non-Christians—or shaky Christians—who could benefit from hearing solid reasons
to believe in God. Not everyone in your group will be interested in scientific evidence, but
they probably know people who doubt God's existence based on scientific-sounding ratio-
nale. So it will be important to help them focus not just on information that helps them, but
also on what might be helpful for people they know. It's natural to focus on their own needs,
but this is a chance to help them get beyond themselves and to become prepared to "give an
answer to everyone who asks" for reasons related to their faith (1 Peter 3:15 NIV).

Question 2. This is a discussion question. If you have time, people can take a moment
to think and jot down their thoughts before they discuss, but mainly the purpose of this
question is to get them to start thinking about how to communicate with friends on these
various paths.

Question 3. Allow about five minutes of silence for people to read these four arrows.
When most people seem finished, move on to discuss question 4.

Question 4. You probably won't have time to discuss each of the arrows in equal depth.
However, just the process of reflecting on even one or two of them will help group members

develop the skills of thinking about a logical argument for faith and reflecting on how different arguments seem more compelling to different people. Group members don't have to fully digest all of these arguments during your meeting, as they can read about them more fully in *Choosing Your Faith* or the other resources listed at the end of session 7.

As the leader, you should try to read the full versions of the arrows in chapters 9–11 of *Choosing Your Faith*. Then, if group members have trouble understanding or seeing the relevance of one of the arrows, you will be able to point them quickly to the fuller explanation in the book. Also, if some of the arrows not listed in the workbook seem especially significant to you, you can talk about them, as well.

Question 5. Give people several minutes of silence to think about what they might do. Again, while they might not personally feel a need for evidence, this exercise will help them take the focus off themselves so they can think about reaching others they know.

If you sense that people don't know what to write, you can invite a discussion of the things that make us hesitant about sharing the evidence with our non-Christian friends. For instance, we might think that our friends who are interested in science know more about it than we do, so they might ridicule us if we raise a scientific issue that we're not prepared to defend articulately. In that case, we need to go into the discussion with a posture that will take into account our lack of scientific expertise, such as: "I learned in a class that the universe is incredibly fine-tuned for life. Do you know anything about that?" Or, "I read something about DNA, and I don't know much about it, but it seemed hard for me to imagine that a code like that could come about by chance. Is that what you believe, that it developed by chance?" We can invite our friend to be the expert, but encourage them to consider new and perhaps challenging information. We can show them what *Choosing Your Faith* says and ask them to comment. It's important for group members to understand that they don't have to become experts in scientific, historical, or other kinds of evidence in order to offer it to people who might be interested in it.

Session 7

The main takeaways from this session are:

- There are reasons other than "God says so" for believing that the Bible is a reliable source of truth.

- There are reasons beyond "the Bible says so" for believing that Jesus really is the Messiah and Son of God.

- We need to think about who in our lives could benefit from knowing these reasons.

Because the DVD for this session is divided into two segments, you'll need to do some time keeping and room managing if you have a large class with many discussion circles. Tell them when they first gather into their discussion circles how much time they have until you'll view the second DVD segment all together.

Eight arrows that point to the Bible and Christ are a lot for most people to think about in one meeting. Feel free to select just a few of them. Group members can read the others on their own. The important things to accomplish in your meeting are ...

- to make people aware that this evidence is readily available;

- to give them the experience of thinking about whether some piece of evidence would be helpful for themselves or for someone they know.

It may not be necessary to completely rearrange the room from discussion circles, to neat rows to view the DVD, and back to discussion circles. It might be faster and easier just to have people turn their chairs for the second DVD segment and then return to their circles for prayer.

Question 2. Arrow 7 speaks of eyewitness accounts. One reference to these eyewitnesses is in 1 Corinthians 15 (it is quoted under "Prayer" at the end of session 7). Two more biblical references to eyewitness accounts are:

> *Many people have set out to write accounts about the events that have been fulfilled among us. They used the eyewitness reports circulating among us from the early disciples. Having carefully investigated everything from the beginning, I also have decided to write a careful account for you, most honorable Theophilus, so you can be certain of the truth of everything you were taught. (Luke 1:1–4)*

> *We proclaim to you the one who existed from the beginning, whom we have heard and seen. We saw him with our own eyes and touched him with our own hands. He is the Word of life. This one who is life itself was revealed to us, and we have seen him. And now we testify and proclaim to you that he is the one who is eternal life. He was with the Father, and then he was revealed to us. We proclaim to you what we ourselves have actually seen and heard so that you may have fellowship with us. (1 John 1:1–3)*

Popular books are published from time to time that claim to prove that the New Testament isn't really based on eyewitness accounts. You might ask your group if any of them have read one of these books or know someone who has read one. If so, there are good books available that rebut this so-called proof. We recommend some examples of books that might be helpful at the end of Session 7.

Question 3. Encourage group members to think of specific people they know—Christians or non-Christians—who would benefit from thinking about this evidence or any of the earlier information we've discussed. Encourage them to watch for natural opportunities to share something they've learned with a friend. For instance, Jesus' sinless life is compelling for many people who might not immediately understand the importance of his sacrificial death. Do you know any non-Christians who might be open to a conversation about the kind of person Jesus was—so ethical in his personal life that even his enemies couldn't come up with faults about which to accuse him?

Session 8

As this is your last meeting in this series, consider doing something to celebrate completing this study. You might ask someone to bring some especially nice refreshments to share at the end of your meeting. You might take time at the end of your meeting to invite group members to share what they've gotten out of the study.

Thank each person for what they have contributed to the study. Give some thought ahead of time to what you might say. Try to remember an insight someone shared, or someone's willingness to engage with new ideas, or even someone's honest disagreement. You can offer this thanks at the beginning of your meeting or at your prayer time.

The main takeaways from this session are:

- Our friends face a variety of barriers as they consider faith in Christ, and many of these barriers are more emotional and spiritual than intellectual. The Holy Spirit can work through us to help our friends across these barriers.

- It's important for us to make ourselves available to help our friends in this way and to keep encouraging them to take steps forward in their spiritual journeys.

After you turn off the DVD and move to your smaller circles for discussion, take turns reading aloud the ten barriers to faith listed under the heading "After the DVD." Make sure everyone understands what the barriers are.

Question 2. Discuss this together. It is a good chance to learn about one another and to make the barriers clear with examples.

Questions 3–4. Give group members about five minutes on their own to write answers for question 3. When most of them seem finished, invite them to share which barriers they listed (question 4). How much variety is there in the group? Do several people note the same barriers?

Question 5. Before question 5 is a list of ideas for helping friends across the various barriers to faith in Christ. Give group members a few minutes to read these silently, especially the ideas for the barriers they think the non-Christians in their lives are facing. Then open up the discussion of question 5. How effective do group members think the suggested ideas would be? Do they have additional ideas? Help each other brainstorm what else they might do to help their friends.

Question 6. Busyness may be the main obstacle people name. It's a genuine problem, as most of us are so busy we hardly have time to rest and invest in friendships with people who are spiritually like minded and therefore encouraging to be around, let alone build friendships with people who see the world very differently from us and may therefore be more challenging. Fear is another obstacle people may be less able or willing to articulate. Fear of failure, fear of the unknown, and even fear of "contaminating" ourselves through exposure to values and behaviors we don't approve of—these are common issues.

Question 7. You can start to address the obstacles you identified in question 6 by committing to face them and pray about them, and by teaming up with one or more individuals or couples in your group. Look at your schedules together. How can you make time for friendship with each other and include one or more non-Christians in a shared meal, family activities, a sporting event, or another area of common interest? It's through simple steps like these that we can begin to deepen friendships, trust, and conversations with the people in our lives who most need the love and truth of Christ.

Some group members may resist teaming up to reach unbelievers. They may have enjoyed the study but may feel they are too busy or uncomfortable to invite unbelievers they barely know to anything. Have an honest discussion about that. Maybe they don't know any non-Christians but would be willing to at least take some initial steps to get to know some. You can at least raise that fact to their awareness. And if even a few group members are willing to share a meal with each other and a few non-Christians, that's progress.

NOTES

Session 1

1. This section was adapted from Mark Mittelberg's chapter "Why Faith in Jesus Matters" in the book *God Is Great, God Is Good*, edited by William Lane Craig and Chad Meister (Downers Grove, IL: InterVarsity, 2009).

Session 5

1. Norman L. Geisler, *Baker Encyclopedia of Christian Apologetics* (Grand Rapids, MI: Baker, 1999), 702.

Session 6

1. Francis S. Collins, *The Language of God: A Scientist Presents Evidence for Belief* (New York: Free Press, 2006), 1–2.

Session 7

1. Dr. Michael Rydelnik, quoted in Lee Strobel, *The Case for Christ: The Film* (Lionsgate Home Entertainment, 2007).

ACKNOWLEDGMENTS

A special thanks to Karen Lee-Thorp for applying her formidable skills in writing, editing, and analysis—as well as her love for truth and heart for ministry—to help shape and complete this teaching series.